Eyewitness

ROCK &

MINERAL

Slice from
septarian nodule

Garnet-chlorite schist

Cinnabar

Hematite

Granite

Gypsum desert rose

Wenlock limestone
with triolobite fossils

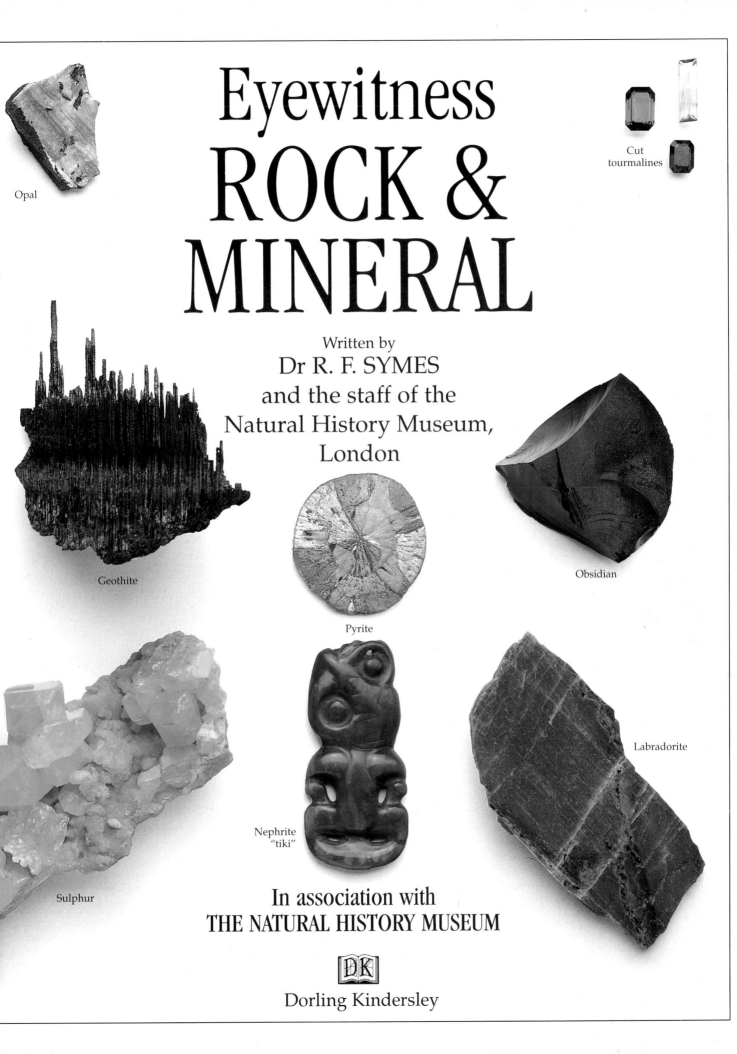

Opal

Cut
tourmalines

Eyewitness
ROCK &
MINERAL

Written by
Dr R. F. SYMES
and the staff of the
Natural History Museum,
London

Geothite

Pyrite

Obsidian

Labradorite

Nephrite
"tiki"

Sulphur

In association with
THE NATURAL HISTORY MUSEUM

DK

Dorling Kindersley

Magnifying lens

LONDON, NEW YORK, MUNICH,
MELBOURNE, and DELHI

Project editor Janice Lacock
Art editor Neville Graham
Managing art editor Jane Owen
Special photography Colin Keates (Natual History
Museum, London) and Andreas Einsiedel
Editorial consultants
Dr R. F. Symes (Natural History Museum, London)
and Dr Wendy Kirk (University College London)

PAPERBACK EDITION
Managing editor Andrew Macintyre
Managing art editor Jane Thomas
Editor and reference compiler Angela Wilkes
Art editor Catherine Goldsmith
Production Jenny Jacoby
Picture research Angela Anderson
DTP designer Siu Yin Ho

Mixed rough
and polished
pebbles

This Eyewitness ® Guide has been conceived by
Dorling Kindersley Limited and Editions Gallimard

Hardback edition first published in Great Britain in 1988.
This edition published in Great Britain in 2002
by Dorling Kindersley Limited,
80 Strand, London WC2R ORL

A CIP catalogue record for this book is
available from the British Library.

ISBN 0 7513 4742 6

Colour reproduction by
Colourscan, Singapore
Printed in Hong Kong by Toppan

See our complete catalogue at

www.dk.com

Chisel

Geologist's hammer

Chalcedony cameo

Contents

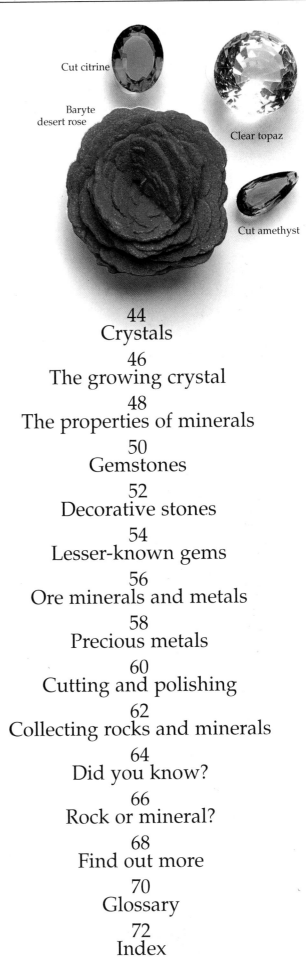

Cut citrine

Baryte
desert rose

Clear topaz

Cut amethyst

6
The Earth

8
What are rocks and minerals?

10
How rocks are formed

12
Weathering and erosion

14
Rocks on the seashore

16
Igneous rocks

18
Volcanic rocks

20
Sedimentary rocks

22
Limestone caves

24
Metamorphic rocks

26
Marble

28
The first flint tools

30
Rocks as tools

32
Pigments

34
Building stones

36
The story of coal

38
Fossils

40
Rocks from space

42
Rock-forming minerals

44
Crystals

46
The growing crystal

48
The properties of minerals

50
Gemstones

52
Decorative stones

54
Lesser-known gems

56
Ore minerals and metals

58
Precious metals

60
Cutting and polishing

62
Collecting rocks and minerals

64
Did you know?

66
Rock or mineral?

68
Find out more

70
Glossary

72
Index

The Earth

Early view of Earth with a central fire

ONE OF THE NINE planets that revolve around the Sun, the Earth is thought to be about 4,600 million years old. Geology literally means "discourse about the Earth". Because rocks can provide valuable information about the Earth in previous times, geologists study them and deduce the processes and events that produced them. As man can currently bore only a few kilometres into the crust, we cannot sample rocks from the mantle directly. The rocks and minerals shown here come from a wide range of environments, and introduce important features that are explained in more detail later in the book.

THE STRUCTURE OF THE EARTH

The Earth consists of three major parts: the core, the mantle and the crust. The crust and upper mantle form continental and oceanic "plates" that move slowly over the mantle beneath. The closer to the centre of the Earth, the greater the temperature and pressure.

Crust, 6-70 km (4-44 miles) thick

Solid mantle, approximately 2,900 km (1,800 miles) thick

Molten outer core, approximately 2,300 km (1,430 miles) radius

Solid inner core, approximately 1,200 km (750 miles) radius

Basaltic magma from the mantle

Continental plate

Oceanic plate

Oceanic ridge

Volcanic range

MOVING PLATES

Where plates collide, mountain ranges like the Himalayas may form. In the ocean, material from the mantle fills the gap between plates to form a ridge. In other areas, oceanic plates are forced down beneath continental plates, causing volcanic activity.

PRECIOUS METALS
Platinum, silver and gold are valuable, rare metals. *For more information, see pp. 58-59.*

SEASHORE PEBBLES
These are formed by the weathering of larger rocks by wave action. *For more information, see pp. 14-15.*

Gold in quartz vein

CRYSTAL HABITS
The shape and size of a crystal is known as its habit. *For more information, see pp. 46-47.*

Cubes of pyrite

MINERAL ORES
These are the source of most useful metals. *For more information, see pp. 56-57.*

Cut citrine, a variety of quartz

Cassiterite, tin ore, from Bolivia

Diamond in kimberlite

GEMSTONES
Rare, hard-wearing and attractive minerals may be cut as gemstones. They are mainly used in jewellery. *For more information, see pp. 50-55.*

Quartz crystals from France

CRYSTALS
Many minerals form regular-shaped solids with flat surfaces, known as crystals. *For more information, see pp. 44-47.*

Shelly limestone

FOSSILS
These rocks contain the remains of, or impressions made by, former plants or animals. *For more information, see pp. 38-39.*

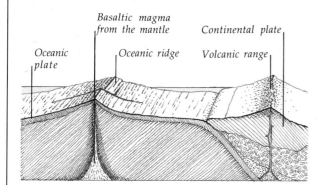

Quartzite beach pebbles

IGNEOUS ROCKS
The most common types of rocks have formed from molten magma. *For more information, see pp. 16-17.*

Granite

VOLCANIC ROCKS
Volcanic activity produces a number of different types of rocks and lava. *For more information, see pp. 18-19.*

Hawaiian ropy lava

Delta
Suez Canal
City of Cairo
River Nile

SATELLITE PICTURE OF RIVER NILE AND DELTA
The River Nile carries rock debris eroded from rocks in central Egypt and deposits it in the delta and sea, where it may eventually form sedimentary rocks (pp. 11 and 20).

Carboniferous Limestone

SEDIMENTARY ROCKS
This group of rocks is formed from compacting sediment produced by the erosion of other rocks. *For more information, see pp. 20-23.*

Anthracite, the hardest form of coal

COAL
A sedimentary rock, coal has formed from the fossilized remains of plants. *For more information, see pp. 36-37.*

Ingito Hills on edge of East African Rift Valley
Lake Amboseli, a dry lake
Chyulu mountain range, Kenya

Mount Meru
Mount Kilimanjaro
Pangani River valley
Glaciers of Kibo

LANDSAT IMAGE OF EAST AFRICA
This area shows a range of landscapes, formed from different rocks. For example, volcanic rocks (p. 18) forming volcanic Mount Kilimanjaro, and evaporites (p. 21) in dried-up lakes.

7

What are rocks and minerals?

ROCKS ARE NATURAL AGGREGATES or combinations of one or more minerals. Some rocks, such as quartzite (pure quartz) and marble (pure calcite) contain only one mineral. Most, however, consist of more than one kind. Minerals are naturally occurring inorganic solids with definite chemical compositions and an ordered atomic arrangement. Here, two common rocks - granite and basalt - are shown along with individual specimens of the major minerals of which they are formed. Rock-forming minerals can be divided into several groups - these are described in more detail on pages 42-43.

James Hutton (1726-97), one of the founders of modern geology

GRANITE AND ITS MAJOR CONSTITUENT MINERALS

Usually, several kinds of minerals are present in a rock, their size and texture varying according to how the rock formed. In the coarse-grained, igneous rock, granite, the three major constituent minerals are visible to the naked eye. They are quartz (grey areas), feldspars (pink and white) and mica (black).

Quartz

Mica

Feldspar

Etched face

1 QUARTZ

Well-developed quartz crystals, like this group, may have milky, etched faces.

2 MICA

Black biotite (a form of mica) crystals can be split into wafer-thin sheets.

3 FELDSPAR

Crystals of orthoclase (a feldspar) may be milky white or pale pink.

BASALT AND ITS MAJOR CONSTITUENT MINERALS

Basalt consists mainly of three minerals - olivine, pyroxene and plagioclase feldspar. However, because it is fine-grained, it is not always possible to distinguish them with the naked eye. This olivine basalt was collected from the crater of the Kilauea volcano in Hawaii.

1 OLIVINE

Transparent green crystals of olivine are comparatively rare, and are known as peridot (p. 54).

2 FELDSPAR

Flat or polished crystals of labradorite, a plagioclase feldspar from Labrador, North America, display a beautiful play of colours.

Iridescent blue and orange visible on the surface

Augite crystal

Rock matrix

3 PYROXENE

This well-developed, single black crystal of augite (a pyroxene) comes from Italy. Augite crystals are found in various igneous rocks.

The scope of rock forms

Rocks and minerals occur in many diverse forms. Rocks do not necessarily have to be hard and resistant - loose sand and wet clay are considered to be rocks. The individual size of minerals in a rock ranges from millimetres, in a fine-grained volcanic rock, to several metres in a granite pegmatite.

ROCKS FORMED WITHIN ROCKS

This sedimentary rock specimen is a claystone septarian nodule. Nodules such as this are formed when groundwater re-distributes minerals within a rock in a particular nodular pattern. Nodules are sometimes known as "concretions". Here, the pattern of veins is formed of calcite.

CRYSTALS FROM MINERAL ORE

Orange-red tabular crystals of the mineral wulfenite from Arizona, U.S.A., are formed in lead- and molybdenum-bearing ore veins.

Eruption of Mount Pelée, Martinique, on 5th August, 1851

ROCKS FROM VOLCANIC ERUPTION

Despite its extraordinary appearance, "Pele's hair" is technically a rock. It consists of golden-brown hair-like fibres of basalt glass which occasionally enclose minute olivine crystals, and was formed from the eruption of basaltic magma as a lava spray.

ROCKS FORMED BY EVAPORATION

Stalactites are formed from substances that are deposited when dripping water evaporates (p. 22). This spectacular blue-green stalactite is composed entirely of the mineral chalcanthite (copper sulphate) and formed from percolating copper-rich waters in a mine.

Section of a mine roof coloured with deposits of the copper mineral, chalcanthite

Lighter bands of pyroxene and plagioclase feldspar

Dark layer of chromite

ROCKS THAT FORM IN LAYERS

Norite is an igneous rock composed of the minerals pyroxene, plagioclase feldspar and the chromium-rich mineral chromite. In this specimen from South Africa, the dark and light minerals have separated from each other so that the rock is layered. The dark chromite layers constitute an important source of chromium.

How rocks are formed

GEOLOGICAL PROCESSES work in constant cycles - redistributing the chemical elements, minerals and rocks within and at the surface of the Earth. The processes that occur within the Earth, such as metamorphism and mountain building, are driven by the Earth's internal heat. Surface processes, such as weathering, are activated by the Sun's energy.

Andesite formed from a volcanic eruption in the Solomon Islands in the Pacific

VOLCANIC ACTIVITY

When rocks of the crust and upper mantle melt, they form magma which may be extruded at the Earth's surface by volcanic activity. The resultant rocks are extrusive igneous rocks (p. 16). The most common example is basalt.

Pure quartz sand formed from weathered granites or sandstones

Basaltic lava from a lava flow in Hawaii

VOLCANIC LANDMARK
Le Puy de Dôme, France, is a plug that was once the central core of an ancient volcano.

Gabbro, the coarse-grained equivalent of basalt, from Finland

IGNEOUS INSELBERG
Sugar Loaf Mountain, Brazil, consists of intrusive igneous rocks that have eventually reached the surface when overlying rocks were weathered away.

Volcanic activity

Weathering

Surface

Igneous rocks

Melting

Magm

Migmatite from Finland

Granite, containing large crystals of pink feldspar, from northern England

MELTING *right*
Occasionally, high temperatures and pressures cause rocks to partially melt. If the rock is then squeezed, snake-like veins may form. Migmatites are mixed rocks consisting of a metamorphic host, such as gneiss or schist, cut by veins of granite. They demonstrate the passage of rocks from the metamorphic state to the molten or igneous.

ROCKS FROM MAGMA

Rocks formed within the Earth from molten magma are called intrusive igneous rocks (p. 16). They are also known as plutonic, after Pluto, the Greek god of the underworld. One such rock, granite, can form enormous masses called "batholiths" in mountain belts.

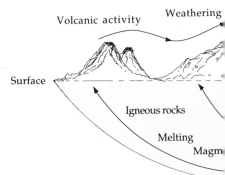

WEATHERING

As the weather acts on rocks it may lead to chemical changes or cause the rocks to fragment (p. 12) and form sediments. For example, sand grains are produced when quartz-bearing rocks are broken down, whilst clays form from weathered feldspar-rich rocks.

Clays produced by weathering become important components of soils

DEPOSITION OF SEDIMENTS

Sediments are transported by rivers, or by the wind in desert regions. Eventually where the speed of the transporting medium slows, as when a river runs into a lake, the sediment is deposited into layers of different sized particles. When these are compacted, they form sedimentary rocks (p. 20).

Layered sandstone from Arkansas, U.S.A.

RIVER TRANSPORT

Rivers such as these (seen from space) transport rock fragments from one area to another. The Mississippi alone deposits thousands of tonnes of debris into its delta each day.

Banded claystone from Uganda

THE ROCK CYCLE

There is no starting point in this cycle which has been going on for millions of years.

Transport

Deposition

Heat and pressure

Metamorphic rocks

Sedimentary rocks

200-million-year-old desert sandstone from Scotland

METAMORPHIC ROCKS

Quartz veins stand out in this schist rock face in Scotland, an area rich in metamorphic rocks.

Quartzite, an altered sandstone, formed by pressure and heat beneath the Earth's surface

Granite

Gneiss

Gneiss, a banded metamorphic rock

Mica schist formed from metamorphosed claystones

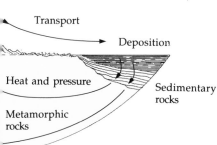

METAMORPHISM

The deeper a rock is within the Earth, the greater the pressure exerted on it from the overlying rocks, and the higher the temperature. Pressure and heat cause the rocks to change or "metamorphose" as the minerals recrystallize. The new rocks are termed metamorphic rocks (p. 24).

Weathering and erosion

ALL ROCKS BREAK DOWN at the Earth's surface. When rocks break down without movement (as they stand) this is called weathering. Weathering is either chemical or mechanical. If rocks break down during movement or by a moving medium, such as a river or glacier, this is called erosion.

Wind erosion

Constant attack by sediment-laden wind may slowly grind away at a rock and erode it.

MONUMENT VALLEY, ARIZONA, U.S.A.
Large-scale abrasion by the wind produces large, protruding landforms called "buttes".

ABRASION BY THE WIND
The abrasive action of the wind wears away softer layers of rock and leaves the harder ones protruding, as in this desert rock from Somalia.

SAND BLASTING
Faceted desert pebbles, formed by sand constantly being blown against them, are called "dreikanters".

Weathering caused by temperature fluctuations

The expansion and contraction of rock as the temperature varies causes it to break up. Also, frost shattering may be caused by expansion of water in the rock as it freezes.

Sandstone composed of sand accumulated 200 million years ago in a desert environment

Sand from a present day desert in Saudi Arabia

DESERT EROSION
Rocks formed in desert conditions, where sediment is carried by wind, are often reddish in colour and composed of characteristically rounded sand grains.

DESERT ENVIRONMENT
Wind and temperature changes cause continual weathering and bizarre, barren landscapes in the Sahara Desert.

ONION-SKIN WEATHERING
In this type of weathering, changes in temperature cause the surface layers of rock to expand, contract and finally peel away from the underlying rock.

Fine-grained dolerite

Onion-skin weathered dolerite

Peeling layers, reminiscent of onion skins, caused by changes in temperature

Chemical weathering

Only a few minerals can resist weathering by acidic rainwater. Minerals dissolved at the surface may be carried downwards into the soil and underlying rock, and redeposited.

Fresh, unaltered granite

Coarse, weathered granite

ALTERED MINERALS
Granite is split by the expansion of water as it freezes. Its constituent minerals are then chemically altered, producing coarse rock fragments.

GRANITE TORS
Tors, weathered rounded rocks, are formed of the remnants left when the surrounding rocks have been eroded away. This example is on Dartmoor, England.

Gossan altered by percolating groundwater

Secondary minerals

CHEMICAL CHANGES
Chemical weathering of an ore-vein may cause redistribution of minerals. The bright coloured minerals were formed from deposits of dissolved minerals from weathered rocks at higher levels. They are termed "secondary deposits".

TROPICAL WEATHERING
In certain tropical climates, quartz is dissolved and carried away, while feldspars are altered to clay minerals which may accumulate as a thick surface deposit of bauxite (p. 56).

Ice erosion

As glaciers move they pick up fragments of rock which become frozen into the base of the ice. The moving, frozen mass causes further erosion of underlying rocks.

Large rock fragment

Scratches caused by a glacier

PARTHENON, ATHENS, GREECE
Chemicals in the air can react with stone and cause drastic weathering. This can be seen on the Parthenon and on some church gargoyles.

SCRATCHED ROCK
The deep gouge marks on this limestone from Grindelwald, Switzerland, were caused by abrading rock fragments contained in the glacier that flowed over it.

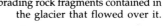

MORTERATSCH GLACIER, SWITZERLAND *left*
Glaciers are a major cause of erosion in mountainous regions.

GLACIER DEPOSITS
A till is a deposit left by a melting glacier, and contains crushed rock fragments ranging from microscopic grains to large pebbles. Ancient tills which have become consolidated into a hard rock are called "tillite". This specimen is from the Flinders Range in South Australia, an area which was glaciated some 600 million years ago.

13

Rocks on the seashore

AT THE SEASHORE, geological processes can be seen taking place. Many seashores are backed by cliffs, beneath which is a deposit of coarse material that has fallen from above. This is gradually broken up by the sea, and sorted into pebbles, gravel, sand and mud. Then the various sizes of sediment are deposited separately - this is the raw material for future sedimentary rocks (p. 20).

Pebbles on Chesil Beach, England

GRADED GRAINS
On the beach, these pebbles are sorted by wave and tide action. The sand comes from a nearby area. It is pure quartz, the other rock-forming minerals having been washed away by constant wave movement.

Large, coarse pebbles

Irregularly shaped pyrite nodule

Mica schist

Slates

SKIMMING STONES
As every schoolboy knows, the best stones for skimming are disc-shaped. They are most likely to be sedimentary or metamorphic rocks, as they split easily into sheets.

LOCAL STONES
These pebbles reflect the local geology, all coming from the rocks of the immediate neighbourhood of the beach where they were collected. They are metamorphic rocks that have been worn into flat discs.

HIDDEN CRYSTALS
Pyrite nodules are common in chalk areas. They may develop interesting shapes. The dull outside breaks to reveal unexpected, radiating crystals inside.

SHELLY PEBBLES
Uninhabited sea shells are subjected to continuous wave action. In time, the sharp edges of broken shells may become smoothed and form pebbles. These are from a beach in New Zealand.

AMBER PEBBLES
Amber is the fossil resin of extinct coniferous trees that lived thousands of years ago. It is especially common along the Baltic coasts of Russia and Poland.

PRESERVED WAVES
Ripple marks and other similar structures form under water from sand carried by currents, and can be seen on many beaches at low tide. In this Finnish specimen, ripple marks are preserved in sandstone, indicating that similar sedimentary processes to those of the present took place in the past (p. 20).

BLACK SANDS

In areas of volcanic activity, beach sand may be rich in dark minerals and often no quartz is present. The olivine sand comes from Raasay, Scotland, while the magnetite-bearing sand is from Tenerife.

Dark olivine sand

Magnetite-bearing sand

Black volcanic ash beach on north coast of Santorini, Greece

Medium-sized, coarse pebbles

Small, fine pebbles

Finest pebbles

Quartz sand

Nodule of marcasite with nobbly exterior

Interior of marcasite reveals glistening crystals radiating outwards

DISCOVERED IN CHALK

Because flint nodules are hard, they resist abrasion and so may be seen concentrated on beaches in Chalk areas, such as those below the famous White Cliffs of Dover, England.

Chalk cliffs often produce pyrite and flint nodules

GRANITIC ORIGIN

In granite country, beach pebbles tend to be of quartz, which is an abundant vein mineral, or pink or grey granite.

Flint nodules from below Chalk cliffs

FOREIGN MATERIAL

Not all beach rocks are of local derivation. This porphyritic igneous rock was probably carried across the North Sea from Norway to England by ice during the last Ice Age.

Assorted glass pebbles

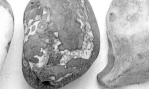

Brick pebble

SYNTHETIC PEBBLES

Apart from the usual natural minerals and rocks, man-made objects may be washed ashore, possibly from ships' ballast, or dumped on the beach. Some of them may eventually become abraded and rounded by wave action.

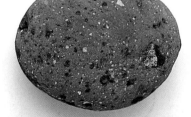

PROTECTING THE BEACH

Artificial groynes stop pebbles and sand drifting.

Igneous rocks

Basalt needle, St Helena

THESE ROCKS are formed when molten magma from deep within the Earth's crust and upper mantle (p. 6) cools and solidifies. There are two types: "intrusive" and "extrusive". Intrusive rocks solidify within the Earth's crust and only appear at the surface after the overlying rocks have been eroded away. Extrusive rocks are formed when magma erupts from a volcano as lava, and cools on reaching the surface.

BASALT COLUMNS
When basaltic lava cools, it often forms hexagonal columns. This spectacular example is the Giant's Causeway in Northern Ireland.

Biotite granite

Graphic granite

Pink granite

Black grains are biotite, a form of mica (p. 42)

Long, angular quartz crystals look like ancient writing against the larger pale-pink feldspar crystals

Pink colouring due to the high proportion of potassium feldspar in the rock

GRANITE
An extemely common intrusive rock, granite consists mainly of coarse grains of quartz, feldspar and mica (p. 8). The individual grains are large because they formed as the magma cooled slowly deep in the earth. Although generally of a mottled appearance, granite samples vary in colour from grey to red according to the different proportions of constituent minerals. Granite is found in many parts of the world. The biotite granite shown here comes from Hay Tor, an outcrop at the highest point on Dartmoor in southwest England (p. 13).

PITCHSTONE
Formed when volcanic lava cools very quickly, pitchstone contains some small crystals of feldspar and quartz and has a dull, resin-like appearance. Pitchstone may be brown, black or grey, and large crystals of feldspar and quartz may be visible.

OBSIDIAN
Like pitchstone, obsidian is a glass formed from rapidly cooled lava. It forms so quickly that there is no time for crystals to grow. The sharp edges shown on this sample from Iceland are characteristic of obsidian, hence its use as an early tool (p. 29).

Olivine

Pyroxene

Plagioclase feldspar

GABBRO
An intrusive rock, gabbro consists of dark minerals such as olivine and augite. It has coarse grains as large crystals formed when the magma slowly cooled. This sample is from the Isle of Skye, Scotland.

Phenocryst of feldspar

FELDSPAR PORPHYRY
Porphyries are rocks that contain large crystals called "phenocrysts" within a medium-grained rock. This particular sample contains feldspar crystals and comes from Wales.

THIN SECTION OF GABBRO
When a very thin slice of rock is viewed under a microscope using a particular kind of light, hidden features, such as crystal shape, are revealed (p. 42). Here, the highly coloured grains are ferromagnesian minerals called olivine and pyroxene, and the grey mineral is plagioclase feldspar.

Vesicular basalt

Empty vesicles or holes

Amygdaloidal basalt

BASALT
Formed from solidified lava, basalt is the most common extrusive rock. It is similar in composition to gabbro but has finer grains. When the lava cools, it may split into many-sided columns. Among the most well-known of these spectacular structures are The Needle on St Helena and the Giant's Causeway in Ireland.

Hole filled with calcite

VESICULAR VOLCANIC ROCKS
Both rocks are basalts that were formed when bubbles of gas were trapped in hot lava scum. The vesicular basalt is light and full of holes known as "vesicles". In amygdaloidal basalt, the holes were later filled in with minerals such as calcite. These rocks were collected from Hawaii, an area of great volcanic activity.

PERIDOTITE
A dark, heavy rock mainly containing minerals called olivine and pyroxene, peridotite is presumed to underlie layers of gabbro 10 km (6 miles) beneath the ocean floor. This sample was found in Odenwald, West Germany.

Green olivine crystals

Dark pyroxene crystals

Calcite vein

SERPENTINITE
As its name suggests, the dominant mineral in this coarse-grained, red and green rock is serpentine. It is streaked with white veins of calcite. Serpentinite is common in the Alps.

Volcanic rocks

ROCKS THAT ARE FORMED by volcanic activity can be divided into two groups: pyroclastic rocks, and acid and basic lavas. Pyroclastic rocks are formed from either solid rock fragments or plastic bombs of lava blown out of the throat of a volcano. The bombs solidify as they fly through the air. Rocks formed from solidified lavas vary according to the type of lava. Acid lavas are thick and sticky, flow very slowly and form steep-sided volcanoes. The more fluid, basic lavas form flatter volcanoes or may well up through cracks in the sea floor. Basic lavas are fast-flowing and so quickly spread out to cover vast areas.

Ejection of lava from Eldfell, Iceland, in 1973

Pyroclastic rocks

Pyroclastic means "fire-broken", an apt name for rocks which consist of rock and lava pieces that were blown apart by exploding gases.

Agglomerate formed close to a vent

VOLCANIC BOMBS
When blobs of lava are thrown out of a volcano, some solidify in the air, landing on the ground as hard "bombs". These two specimens are shaped like rugby footballs, but bombs may be spherical or irregular in appearance.

Intrusion breccia formed within a vent

JUMBLED PIECES
The force of an explosion may cause rocks to fragment. As a result, a mixture of angular pieces often fills the central vent or is laid down close to vents. The fragments form rocks known as agglomerates.

Ash

INSIDE A VOLCANO
Magma flows through a central vent or escapes through side vents. Underground it may form dykes that cut across rock layers, and sills of hardened magma parallel to rock strata.

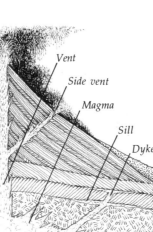

Vent

Side vent

Magma

Sill

Dyke

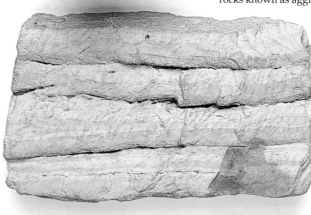

Bedded tuff (a hardened ash)

WIND-BLOWN PARTICLES
Tiny fragments of volcanic ash can travel for thousands of kilometres in the atmosphere. Where it settles and hardens it forms tuff. This ash erupted from Mount St Helens, in northwest U.S.A., in 1980. The coarse grains were blown five km (three miles) from the crater, while the fine particles were wind-carried for 27 km (17 miles).

Eruption of Mount St Helens, 1980

Acid lavas

Viscous, acid lavas move slowly and may solidify in the volcano's vent, thereby trapping gases. As pressure builds up, these may explode to form pyroclastic rocks.

ERUPTION OF VESUVIUS
The famous eruption in 79 AD produced a *nuée ardente*, a fast-moving cloud filled with magma and ash. The Roman town of Pompeii was destroyed in this event.

Aphthitalite

Aphthitalite

ROCKS FROM GASES
Inactive volcanoes are said to be "dormant". Even when volcanoes are dormant or dying, volcanic gases may escape and hot springs form. These colourful rocks were formed in this way at Vesuvius.

DESTRUCTION OF AKROTIRI
This Minoan town on Santorini was buried by volcanic ash, c. 1450 BC.

FLOATING ROCKS
Pumice is solidified lava froth. Because the froth contains bubbles of gas, the rock is peppered with holes, like a honeycomb. Pumice is the only rock that floats in water. This sample is from the Lipari Islands, Italy.

NATURAL GLASS
Although chemically the same as pumice, obsidian (p. 16) has a totally different glassy texture. Because of its sharp edges, primitive man used it for tools, arrowheads and ornaments (p. 29).

TREACLE-LIKE LAVAS
This light-coloured, fine-grained rock is called rhyolite. The distinctive bands formed as the sticky, viscous lava flowed for short distances.

Basic lavas

These lavas flow smoothly, and may cover vast distances with a thin layer. As a result, the vent does not get choked and gases can escape, so that although there is plenty of lava, few pyroclastic rocks are formed.

RUNNY LAVAS
Basaltic lavas are fast-flowing and so quickly spread out to cover vast areas. This specimen of basalt (p. 17) was deposited by the Hualalai Volcano, one of the many volcanoes on Hawaii.

MULTI-COLOURED BASALT
Sparkling points in this basalt include green olivine and black pyroxene crystals.

WRINKLED ROCKS
When lava flows, the surface cools and forms a skin, which wrinkles as the fluid centre carries on flowing. The resulting rocks are called ropy lavas.

Sedimentary rocks

W HEN ROCKS are weathered and eroded (p. 12) they break down into smaller pieces of rock and minerals. This material, which is called sediment, may eventually be transported to a new site, often in the sea or in river beds. The sediments are deposited in layers which become buried and compacted. In time the particles are cemented together to form new rocks, known as sedimentary rocks. In large outcrops it is often possible to see the various layers of sediment with the naked eye.

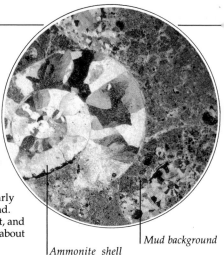

THIN SECTION OF LIMESTONE
Under the microscope (p. 42), fine details in this ammonite limestone are revealed. The ammonite shells (p. 38) show up clearly against the mud background. Ammonites are now extinct, and we know this rock must be about 160 million years old.

Ammonite shell

Mud background

RAW INGREDIENTS *above*
Foraminifera are marine organisms that secrete lime. Although rarely bigger than a pin-head, they play an extremely important part in rock-building. When they die, the shells fall to the ocean floor where they eventually become cemented into limestone.

Shell remains embedded in rock

Chalk

Oolitic limestone

Shelly limestone

Gastropod limestone

Remains of gastropod shell

Rounded grains known as "ooliths"

FLINT
A form of silica (p. 42), lumps of flint are often found in limestones, especially chalk. They are grey or black, but the outside may be covered in a white powder-like material. Like obsidian (p. 16), when flint is broken, it has a "conchoidal" fracture (p. 48).

LIMESTONES
Many sedimentary rocks consist of the remains of once-living organisms. In some, such as these shelly and gastropod limestones, the remains of animals are clearly visible in the rock. However, chalk, which is also a limestone, is formed from the skeletons of tiny sea animals that are too small to see with the naked eye. Another limestone, oolite, forms in the sea as calcite builds up around grains of sand. As the grains are rolled backwards and forwards by waves, they become larger.

ALGAL LIMESTONE
So-called "muddy" limestones like this are often referred to as "landscape marbles". This is because when the minerals crystallize they may produce patterns in the shape of trees and bushes.

Hole-filled, irregular-shaped rock

CALCAREOUS TUFA
An extraordinary looking evaporite, this porous rock is formed by the evaporation of spring water and is sometimes found in limestone caves (p. 22).

EVAPORITES
Some sedimentary rocks are formed from the evaporation of saline waters. Examples of these include gypsum and halite, the latter being more commonly known as rock salt, from which we get table salt. Gypsum is used to make plaster of Paris, and in its massive form is called alabaster. Both halite and gypsum are minerals that can be found in large deposits worldwide at sites where evaporation of sea water has occurred.

Gypsum crystals growing from a central point like daisy petals

Single crystals of rock salt are not found as often as massive samples

Halite

Gypsum

Reddish cast caused by impurities in the salt

GRAND CANYON, U.S.A.
This spectacular scenery was formed by the erosion of red sandstone and limestone.

Grit

Red sandstone

SANDSTONES
Although both these rocks are made by the cementing together of grains of sand, their texture varies. The red sandstone was formed in a desert where the quartz grains were rounded and polished by the wind. The grains in grit are more angular as they were buried quickly, before they could be smoothed by rubbing.

CLAY
Formed of very fine grains that cannot be seen by the naked eye, clay feels sticky when wet. It may be grey, black, white or yellowish. When it is compacted and all the water forced out of it, it forms hard rocks called mudstone or shale.

BEDDED VOLCANIC ASH
In many sedimentary rocks it is possible to distinguish the individual layers of sediments as they form visible bands. Here, the stripes are layers of volcanic ash. The surface has been polished to highlight this feature.

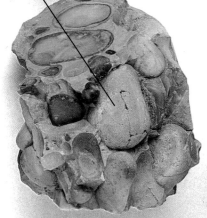

Flint pebble

CONGLOMERATE
The flint pebbles in this rock were rounded by water as they were rolled about at the bottom of rivers or seas. After they were buried, they gradually became cemented together to form a rock known as conglomerate.

Large rock fragment

BRECCIA
Like conglomerate, breccias contain fragments of rock. However, these are much more angular as they have not been rounded by water or carried far from their original home - often the scree (broken rocks) at the bottom of cliffs.

Limestone caves

SPECTACULAR CAVES, lined with dripping stalactites and giant stalagmites are perhaps the best-known of limestone wonders. The caves are formed as a result of slightly acidic rainwater turning the carbonate into bicarbonate and this material is soluble in water and is carried away. In addition to caves, this process also produces several other characteristic features including limestone pavements and karst landscapes.

Top section attached to the roof of cave

Point of intersection

Stalactites of this thickness may take hundreds of years to form

STALACTITES
Stalactites are formed in caves by groundwater containing dissolved lime dripping from the roof and leaving a thin deposit as it evaporates. Growing downwards from the roof, they increase in size by a few millimetres each year and may eventually reach many metres in length. Where the water supply is seasonal, stalactites may show annual growth rings, similar to those of tree trunks.

Single stalactite formed from two smaller ones growing together

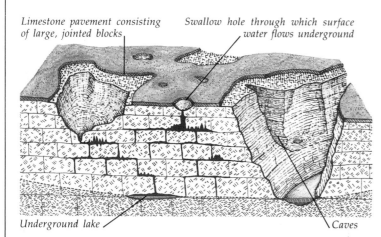

Limestone pavement consisting of large, jointed blocks

Swallow hole through which surface water flows underground

Underground lake

Caves

LIMESTONE LANDSCAPES *above*
Rainwater dissolves calcite in limestone, producing deep, narrow structures ("grikes"). In time, the water percolating down such cracks enlarges them into passages. Although the surface remains dry, flowing water dissolves the rock, producing "swallow holes" at the junctions between grikes. Underground streams flow through caves and form subterranean lakes. Some calcite is re-deposited in the caves to form stalactites and stalagmites.

PLAN DE SALES, FRANCE
Limestone pavements consist of large, cracked, flat blocks ("clints") of rock. They occur where weathering of pure limestone leaves no insoluble residue, such as clay, to make soil.

TUFA
A precipitate, tufa (p. 21) forms when lime is deposited from water onto a rock surface in areas of low rainfall. If a man-made object is left in lime-rich waters it may become coated in tufa.

Coral-like structure

EASE GILL CAVES, ENGLAND
The fine stalactites and stalagmites in this cave form the most spectacular part of a much larger, complex cave system under the hills of the Lancashire Pennines. In fact, this is the largest cave system in the U.K.

Odd-shaped
stalactite

*Prominent growth
rings mark the gradual
development of the
stalactite as successive
deposits formed*

*Point onto which
overhead drips fall*

Orange twin
stalactite

Last section to grow

**STONE FOREST,
CHINA**
The staggering
landscape of the
Hunan Province of
China is typical of
"karst" scenery.
Named after the
limestone area of
Karst in Yugoslavia,
the term is applied
to many limestone
regions, including the
Cumberland Plateau,
U.S.A., parts of the
Blue Mountains,
Australia, and the
Causses, France.

**PAMUKKALE FALLS,
TURKEY**
Beautiful travertine
terraces are formed
from the precipitation
of calcite from hot
springs in limestone
areas. Travertine is
quarried as a
decorative building
stone (p. 27).

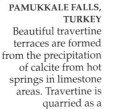

STALAGMITES
Stalagmites are
formed on the floor
of caves where
water has dripped
from the roof or a
stalactite above.
Like stalactites,
they develop as
water containing
dissolved lime
evaporates.
Stalactites and
stalagmites can
grow together
and meet to form
pillars. These
have been de-
scribed as "organ
pipes", "hanging
curtains" and
"portcullises".

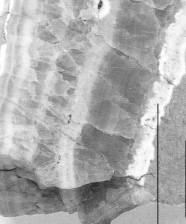

*Colour caused by
impurities in the deposit*

Layer of relatively pure calcite

INSIDE A STALACTITE
This specimen has been sliced through the centre to reveal
coloured bands. The different colours show how the stalactite
formed from deposits of lime with varying degrees of purity.
The purest parts are the whitest.

*End attached to
floor of the cave*

Metamorphic rocks

Schist

THESE ROCKS get their name from the Greek words *meta* and *morphe*, meaning "change of form", and are igneous (p. 16) or sedimentary (p. 20) rocks that have been altered by heat and/or pressure. Such conditions can occur during mountain-building processes (p. 6); buried rocks may then be subjected to high temperatures and may be squeezed or folded, causing minerals in the rocks to recrystallize and new minerals to form. Other metamorphic rocks are formed when rocks surrounding a hot igneous mass are "baked" by the heat.

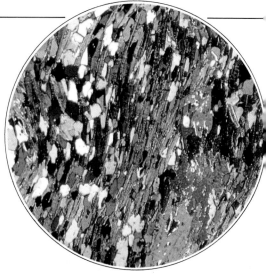

THIN SECTION OF GARNET-MICA SCHIST
Seen through a petrological microscope (p. 42), this Norwegian rock reveals brightly coloured, blade-shaped mica crystals. Quartz and feldspar appear as various shades of grey, while garnet appears black.

Saccharoidal marble

MARBLES
When limestone is exposed to very high temperatures, new crystals of calcite grow and form the compact rock known as marble. It is sometimes confused with the similar-looking rock, quartzite. However, marble is softer and may be easily scratched with a knife. Some medium-grained marble looks sugary and is called "saccharoidal". This specimen comes from Korea. The other two marbles are formed from limestone containing impurites, such as pyroxene.

Evenly sized grains give a sugary appearance

Nodular grey marble

Impure marble

Spotted hornfels

Chiastolite slate

Elongated chiastolite crystals

Aggregates of carbon

Spotted slate

FROM SLATE TO HORNFELS
The irregular speckles in spotted slate are small aggregates of carbon, formed by heat from an igneous intrusion. In rocks nearer the intrusion, the temperature is considerably higher and needle-like crystals of chiastolite form in the slate. The rocks very close to the intrusion become so hot that they completely recrystallize and form a tough, new rock called hornfels.

Garnet-muscovite-chlorite schist

Red garnet crystals

Blue, blade-like crystals of kyanite

Kyanite-staurolite schist

19th-century slate quarry

SLATE
During mountain building, shale was squeezed so hard that the flaky mineral mica recrystallized at right angles to the pressure. The resultant rock, slate, splits easily into thin sheets.

SCHISTS
An important group of metamorphic rocks is termed schist. These medium-grained rocks formed from shale or mud but at a higher temperature than slate. For example, the garnet-muscovite-chlorite schist shown here must have been exposed to temperatures of at least 500°C (932°F) because garnet crystals do not grow at lower temperatures. Kyanite-staurolite schist forms under high pressure, 10-15 km (6-9 miles) below the Earth's surface.

Light coloured layer containing quartz and feldspar

Dark band of biotite

Banded gneiss

Black biotite crystals

Blue kyanite crystals

Biotite-kyanite gneiss

Crystals of a green variety of pyroxene

Red garnet crystals

ECLOGITE
A rock produced under very high pressure, eclogite is extremely dense and is thought to form in the mantle (p. 6) - considerably deeper than most other rocks. It contains pyroxene and small, red crystals of garnet.

GNEISSES
At high temperatures and pressures, igneous or sedimentary rocks may be metamorphosed to gneisses. They have coarser grains than schists and are easily identified because the minerals frequently separate into bands. These layers may be irregular where the rock has been folded under pressure.

MIGMATITE
Under intense heat parts of rocks may start to melt and flow, creating swirling patterns. This is very often shown in migmatites. They are not composed of one rock but a mixture of a dark host rock with lighter coloured granitic rock. This sample is from the Scottish Highlands.

Dark host rock

Pink granitic rock

Marble

STRICTLY SPEAKING, marble is a metamorphosed limestone (p. 24). However, the term "marble" is often used in the stone industry for a variety of other rocks. All are valued for their attractive range of textures and colours, and because they are easily cut and polished. Marble has been widely used for statuary, particularly by the ancient Greeks, while its use in building reached a peak under the Romans.

IN THE RAW *below*
A true marble, this unpolished, coarsely crystalline specimen of Mijas Marble is from Malaga, Spain. Looking at uncut rock it is hard to envisage the patterns a polished sample will reveal.

MEDICI MADONNA
Michelangelo sculpted this statue from Carrara marble, c. 1530.

CARRARA QUARRY
The world's most famous marble comes from the Carrara quarry in Tuscany, Italy. Michelangelo used it as it was the local stone.

ITALIAN SPECIALITY *left*
Grey Bardilla marble comes from Carrara, Italy, an area famous for its marble production.

GREEK CONNECTION
Originally from the Greek Island of Euboea, streaked Cipollino marble is now quarried in Switzerland, the Island of Elba, and Vermont, U.S.A. It was used in the Byzantine church of St Sophia in Istanbul, Turkey.

ITALIAN ELEGANCE *right*
Another striking Italian marble is the black and gold variety from Liguria.

TUSCAN STONES
The distinctive texture of
the Italian decorative stone,
Breccia Violetto, was the reason for
its use in the Paris Opera House in 1875.

TAJ MAHAL
India's most famous monument is
made of assorted marbles.

**SOUTH
AFRICAN SWIRLS**
Polished travertine, a
variety of tufa (pp. 21
and 23) has beautiful
swirling patterns. This
specimen is from Cape
Province, South Africa.

SWISS ORIGINS
The limestone breccia
known as Macchia-
vecchia is quarried in
Mendrisio, Switzerland.

Detail of marble
inlaywork on the
Taj Mahal

AFRICAN COPPER *left*
The vivid colouring of
Green Verdite is caused
by the presence of
copper. It comes
from Swaziland.

ALGERIAN ROCK *bottom*
Breche Sanguine or Red African
is a red breccia (p. 21) from
Algeria. The Romans used
it in the Pantheon, Rome.

The first flint tools

BECAUSE FLINT SPLITS in any direction, fractures to a sharp edge and is fairly wide-spread, it was adopted by primitive people to fashion sharp tools. To begin with these were crude choppers, but gradually more sophisticated weaponry and tools such as scrapers and knives were developed.

Rough flint nodule found in Chalk areas

Leather thong securing flint and antler sleeve to handle

TOOLS FROM FLINT
Flint was shaped by detaching flakes from a nodule to leave a core that gradually became more refined.

Sharp edged tool used for skinning and cutting

STONE-ON-STONE
The earliest tools were made by striking a stone against the flint, to remove chips and leave sharp jagged edges.

PRESSURE-FLAKING
More efficient cutting edges and finer chips were achieved with sharp, pointed implements, such as antler bone.

Scrapers were used to dress animal hides during the Neolithic period

Flint flakes and chippings

Large sharpened handaxe

Cutting edge

Light-coloured handaxe

Small sharpened handaxe

Early men using handaxes

Crude early chopper

Rough cutting edge

HANDAXES
Palaeolithic handaxes were used for smashing animal bones, skinning hunted animals, cutting wood and sometimes even for cutting plants. The well-developed, dark axes are 300,000-70,000 years old. The smaller of the two may once have been larger, being reduced in size by sharpening. The lighter-coloured axe dates to around 70,000-35,000 BC.

Sharp cutting edge

Mesolithic adze

Antler sleeve

Hafted adzes were used to hollow out and shape canoes

DANISH AXE AND DAGGER

This Early Bronze Age axe, found in the River Thames in England, is known to be an imported piece because of its shape. This fact and the careful polish applied to it suggest it would have been a prestigious object. This is also true of the Early Bronze Age flint dagger (2,300-1,200 BC). Its shape imitates the earliest copper daggers, which would initially have been very rare, highly valued items.

Axe

Flint dagger

HAFTED ADZES

Adzes are identified by their asymmetrical cutting edge, and the way they are hafted with the blade at right angles to the handle. They were swung vertically rather than horizontally, and used for shaping wood. These specimens date to the Mesolithic period (10,000-4,000 BC).

Adze mounted directly onto handle

Asymmetrical cutting edge of flint

ARROWHEADS

Although the bow and arrow was first invented in the preceding Mesolithic period, it continued in use for hunting in the Early Neolithic period, when leaf-shaped arrowheads were common. Later, in the Beaker period (2,750-1,800 BC), barbed arrowheads became characteristic. It was a time of change with the introduction of metallurgy.

Neolithic leaf-shaped arrowheads

Beaker-period arrowheads

Reproduction wooden handle

SICKLE

Flint sickles imply the cultivation of crops. The long, slightly curved blade was used to reap crops. Sometimes the sickles have a "gloss" on their cutting edge, which is a polish caused by repeated harvesting. This one, mounted in a reproduction handle, is of Neolithic age (4,000-2,300 BC).

Ninth-century obsidian axe from Mexico

FLINT DAGGERS

These two daggers are also from the Beaker period. Their rarity, and the care with which they were made, suggest they may have served as much as status symbols as weapons.

Reproduction wooden handle

Spearhead with obsidian blade from the Admiralty Islands, off Papua New Guinea

OBSIDIAN

Like flint, obsidian was fashioned into early tools because it fractures with sharp edges. It was even used as a primitive mirror.

Rocks as tools

FLINT WAS NOT THE ONLY ROCK utilized by early people. Archaeologists have found numerous examples of stone implements from many different cultures spanning the world. Some were used as weapons, others as agricultural or domestic tools, ranging from mortars to storage vessels and make-up palettes. Many weapons appear never to have been used, and may have been purely status symbols.

Brazilian stone axe

Neolithic axe showing a highly polished surface

Neolithic axe made of diorite, an igneous rock

Neolithic axe made of rhyolitic tuff, a volcanic rock

STONE AXES

All these stone axes date from the Neolithic period in Britain (4,000-2,300 BC). They are highly polished and tougher than flaked, flint axes. They must have been traded over long distances as the source rocks were hundreds of kilometres from the places where the axes were found.

Wedge to stop the stone moving

Bored quartzite pebble

Reproduction wooden stick

Sharpened wooden point for digging hard ground

Carved stone maul - a war-club or mace - made by Haida Indians, a North American tribe who live on islands off British Columbia

South African digging stick with horn point and stone weight

BATTLE AXES

These perforated axes belong to the Early Bronze Age (2,300-1,200 BC). The top two could have served as weapons but the bottom one is usually described as an "axe-hammer", because one end could have been used as an axe, the other as a hammer. Because they are preserved so well, it is likely that they all would have been just as much for display as for use.

WEIGHTED DIGGING STICK

Pebbles, like this quartzite example, were sometimes pierced and used to weight the end of pointed wooden sticks. During the Mesolithic and Neolithic periods (10,000-2,300 BC) such sticks were used to break up the ground to plant crops or grub up roots.

Breaking up ground with a digging stick prior to planting

Side view of battle axe made of diorite

Top view of battle axe

Dual-purpose granite axe-hammer

Hammer end

Axe end

WHETSTONES
Bronze implements were sharpened by rubbing the blunt edge against an elongated stone. Often the stones were perforated so that they could be hung on a loop around the neck or belt. These whetstones are from the Bronze Age (2,300-700 BC).

Engraved Viking forge stone made of soapstone, used in making metal weapons and tools

A bird-shaped mortar carved by Haida Indians (opposite)

MARBLE MAKE-UP PALETTE
Roman cosmetics included: chalk and powdered lead to whiten the face and arms; red ochre to tint the lips and cheeks; and soot to darken the eyebrows. Using fine bronze or bone spoon-like implements, small amounts were placed on stone palettes and mixed with water or a water-soluble gum. They could then be applied as a paint or paste.

STONE SPINDLE WHORL *right*
The Romans also used stones as spindle whorls. The end of wool or cotton fibres was attached to a bone or wooden spindle weighted with the whorl. As the spindle hung down, its weight and rotating motion helped the twisting of the thread, which was then wound on to the spindle.

Handle

Rotating stone

ROMAN ROTARY QUERN
During Roman times a portable quern was used for grinding corn in the home. It consisted of two stones: the lower one was bedded in earth or fixed to a bench, while the upper stone, held in position by a spindle, was rotated above it by means of the handle. The grain was fed through the hole in the upper stone, the rotary motion forcing it between the grinding surfaces.

Using a stone quern to grind corn during the Iron Age

Grain ready for grinding

Conglomerate stone (p. 21) attached to a bench or bedded in the earth

Pigments

WHEN EARLY MAN started to paint his body and his shelter, he did not have to look far for pigments to colour paints and dyes. By crushing local coloured rocks and mixing the powders with animal fats he produced a range of colours. Over the centuries, as trading routes expanded, new colours were introduced into the artist's palette. The colours of many toxic pigments are now produced synthetically.

Brown clay

Powdered brown clay

Green clay

Powdered green clay

EARTHY HUES
Clays were used extensively by early artists because they were widely available and, being fine-grained, were easily pulverized. They produced mostly drab green and brown colours.

Ochre paint

Umber paint

SHADES OF WHITE
The earliest white pigment was chalk (p. 20), although in some areas kaolin (china clay) was used instead.

Powdered chalk

CAVE PAINTING
The earliest known artworks were executed by cavemen using a mixture of clays, chalk, earths and burnt wood and bones.

COLOUR VARIATION IN A MINERAL
Many minerals are uniformly coloured and the colour can form a useful identification aid. Some, however, exhibit a range of colours. For example, tourmaline (p. 55) may occur as black, brown, pink, green and blue crystals or show a variety of colours in a single crystal.

Chalk White paint

Bison from Grotte de Niaux, France, c. 20,000 BC

COLOUR CLUES
A useful aid in identification is the colour produced when a mineral is finely crushed. The simplest method of achieving this is to scrape the sample gently across an unglazed white tile. Many minerals leave a distinct coloured streak which may or may not be the same colour as the mineral; others crush to a white powder and have no discernible streak.

Orpiment

Cinnabar

Crocoite

Chalcopyrite

Hematite

Molybdenite

Powdered charcoal

BLACK AS COAL
Still popular with artists today, charcoal was well known to cave painters. They found plentiful supplies in the embers of their fires.

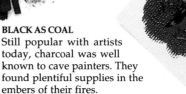

Lamp Black paint

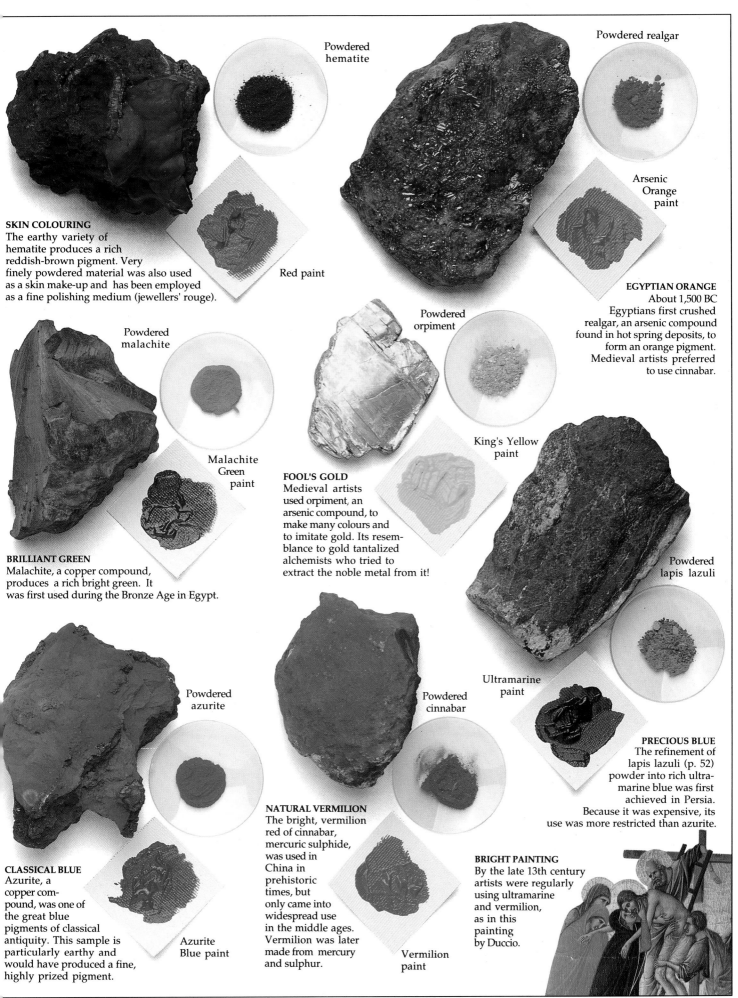

Powdered
hematite

Powdered realgar

SKIN COLOURING
The earthy variety of
hematite produces a rich
reddish-brown pigment. Very
finely powdered material was also used
as a skin make-up and has been employed
as a fine polishing medium (jewellers' rouge).

Red paint

Arsenic
Orange
paint

EGYPTIAN ORANGE
About 1,500 BC
Egyptians first crushed
realgar, an arsenic compound
found in hot spring deposits, to
form an orange pigment.
Medieval artists preferred
to use cinnabar.

Powdered
malachite

Powdered
orpiment

Malachite
Green
paint

King's Yellow
paint

FOOL'S GOLD
Medieval artists
used orpiment, an
arsenic compound, to
make many colours and
to imitate gold. Its resem-
blance to gold tantalized
alchemists who tried to
extract the noble metal from it!

BRILLIANT GREEN
Malachite, a copper compound,
produces a rich bright green. It
was first used during the Bronze Age in Egypt.

Powdered
lapis lazuli

Powdered
azurite

Powdered
cinnabar

Ultramarine
paint

PRECIOUS BLUE
The refinement of
lapis lazuli (p. 52)
powder into rich ultra-
marine blue was first
achieved in Persia.
Because it was expensive, its
use was more restricted than azurite.

CLASSICAL BLUE
Azurite, a
copper com-
pound, was one of
the great blue
pigments of classical
antiquity. This sample is
particularly earthy and
would have produced a fine,
highly prized pigment.

Azurite
Blue paint

NATURAL VERMILION
The bright, vermilion
red of cinnabar,
mercuric sulphide,
was used in
China in
prehistoric
times, but
only came into
widespread use
in the middle ages.
Vermilion was later
made from mercury
and sulphur.

Vermilion
paint

BRIGHT PAINTING
By the late 13th century
artists were regularly
using ultramarine
and vermilion,
as in this
painting
by Duccio.

Building stones

Quarrying in the early 19th century was still done almost entirely by manual labour

Most of the great monuments of the past - the temples and palaces - have survived because they were made from tough, natural stone. Good building stones are relatively easy to work yet must be neither too friable nor prone to splitting and weathering. Today, natural building stones, such as marbles (p. 26), are used mainly as decorative stones, and man-made materials are used for construction.

NUMMULITIC LIMESTONE
This, one of the most famous limestones, is quarried near Cairo, Egypt. It contains many small fossils and was formed about 40 million years ago. The Pyramids were built with stone from the same quarries.

The Pyramids, Egypt, made of local limestone

Fossils

Tooling

PORTLAND STONE
The surface marks on this English limestone are produced by "tooling", a decorative technique which was popular in the last century. After the Great Fire of London in 1666, Portland Stone was used to rebuild St Paul's Cathedral.

OOLITIC LIMESTONE
Formed some 160 million years ago, this limestone is used as a building stone and sometimes in the manufacture of cement.

CHRISTIAN MOSAIC
Small fragments of local stones were often used to make intricate mosaic floors.

Welsh slate

160-million-year-old limestone used for roofing

SLATE
Unlike most building materials, roofing stones must split easily into thin sheets. Slate (p. 25) is ideal. However, where it was not available, builders used local, often inferior, stone for roofing.

NOTRE DAME, PARIS
The famous Parisian cathedral was built from local limestone from the St Jacques region of Paris between 1163 and 1250. Interestingly, the catacombs in Paris are old quarries.

Interlocking roof tile

Pantile

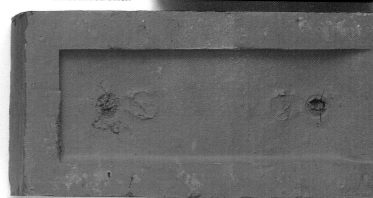

SANDSTONES
Various coloured sandstones make excellent building stones. The French town of Carcassonne is mostly built of sandstone, as are many fine Mogul monuments in India.

Man-made stones

Man is now able to manufacture building stone substitutes such as brick and tiles, cement, concrete and glass. However, all these products originate from rocks of some kind.

ROOFING TILES
In many parts of the world, man-made roofing tiles are moulded and fired from clay.

Textured buff brick

230-million-year-old sandstone

GRANITE
Frequently used to face large buildings, polished granite is also used for headstones. Much of Leningrad, U.S.S.R., including the imperial palaces, is made of imported Finnish granite.

EMPIRE STATE BUILDING, NEW YORK
Although mostly made of granite and sandstone, some man-made materials were used in the construction.

Smooth red brick

Red sandstone from Scotland used as a cladding building stone

GREAT WALL OF CHINA
The 2400 km- (1500 mile-) long Great Wall, the largest single building work on Earth, is built of various materials depending on the terrain it passes through. Sections include brick, granite and various local rocks.

BRICKS
Easily moulded clays are fired to make bricks. Impurities in clays produce bricks of different colours and strengths, making them suitable for a variety of uses.

CEMENT
This is made by grinding and heating a suitable limestone. When mixed with sand, gravel and water, it produces concrete, perhaps the most common building medium today.

The story of coal

THE COAL we burn today is millions of years old. It started off as vegetation in the swampy forests that covered parts of Europe, Asia and North America. As leaves, seeds and dead branches fell on to the wet forest floor, they began to rot. This soft, rotting material later became buried. The weight of the overlying sediments gradually squeezed the water out and compressed the plant material into a solid mass of peat and eventually coal. As pressure and heat increased, five different types of coal were formed in succession.

Plant roots

FOSSILIZED WOOD
Jet is a hard, black material derived from driftwood fragments laid down in the sea. It is very light. Often polished, carved and made into jewellery or decorative objects, jet has been used since the Bronze Age.

"COAL" AS JEWELLERY
A major source of jet is Yorkshire, in northern England. These Roman pendants were found in York and so were almost certainly made of local material.

OIL SHALE
This sedimentary rock is called oil shale because oil can be extracted from it. It contains an organic substance of plant and animal origin called kerogen. When heated, this gives off a vapour from which oil is extracted.

Leaf

Stalk

Seed case

THE ORIGINS OF COAL
Carboniferous swamps may have looked similar to this stylized engraving.

THE RAW INGREDIENTS OF COAL
For coal to form, there must be thick layers of vegetation in areas with poor drainage, such as swamps or bogs. The dead plants become water-logged, and although they start to rot, they cannot decay completely.

THE PEAT LAYER
Peat is a more compact form of the surface layer of rotting vegetation. Some plant roots and seed cases are still visible. In certain parts of the world, where new peat is form-ing today, it is cut and dried, then burnt as a fuel.

CUTTING PEAT
Like their ancestors, many Irish farmers still collect peat using traditional methods.

BROWN COAL
When peat is compressed, it forms a crumbly, brown substance called "lignite" which still contains recognizable plant remains. Whereas 90 per cent of undried peat is water, lignite contains only 50 per cent water.

COAL SEAMS
Layers of coal are called seams. They are sandwiched between layers of other material, such as sandstones and mudstones, which were formed by deposition from rivers. These lignite seams are in a French quarry.

"BLACK GOLD"
Under pressure, lignite is converted into bituminous or household coal. It is hard and brittle and has a very high carbon content. It is dirty to handle as it contains a charcoal-like, powdery substance. A lump of coal may have alternating shiny and dull layers, and recognizable plant material, such as spores.

CONDITIONS IN THE MINES
During the Industrial Revolution, many children were forced to work extremely long hours in appal-ling conditions in underground mines, as this engraving drawn in 1842 shows.

MINING FOR COAL
Man has been mining coal since the Middle Ages. Some mines are open-cast where all the coal is mined at the surface, but most are several hundred metres beneath the land or sea. Now-adays much mechanized equip-ment is used on the coal faces.

THE HARDEST COAL
The highest-quality coal is "anthracite". This shiny substance is harder than other coals and clean to touch. It is the most valuable of all the coals as it contains more carbon than any of the other forms, and it gives out most heat and little smoke.

Fossils

FOSSILS ARE the evidence of past life preserved in the rocks of the Earth's crust. Fossils are formed when an animal or plant is buried in sediment. Usually the soft parts rot away, but the hardest parts remain. This is why most fossils consist of the bones or shells of animals, or the leaves or woody parts of plants. In some marine fossils, shells may be replaced by other minerals or an impression of the insides or outsides may be preserved. Fossils are found in sedimentary rocks, especially limestones and shales. Many fossils are of plants and animals now extinct, such as dinosaurs. They reveal details about the animals and plants that existed millions of years ago, and enable palaeontologists to date the rocks in which they appear. Fossils showing footprints or burrows, rather than remains are called "trace fossils".

Muddy rock

Impression of leaf

Beech leaf

LEAF IMPRINT
This preserved leaf is similar to the modern beech leaf. Even though it is about 40 million years old, much of the original detail and texture can still be seen

Magnolia leaf from Miocene period

Neuropteris - a seed-fern - fossilized in ironstone

PLANT FOSSILS
Many fern-like fossils are found in coal-bearing rocks (p. 36). Formed in the Carboniferous period, they are called "Coal Measures fossils". Although they are not exactly the same botanical species as the ferns that grow today, many are extraordinarily similar.

Fern from the Carboniferous period

Fronds of a fern called *Asterotheca* preserved in stone

Present-day fern

Section of a
Nautilus shell

NAUTILUS
Like the ammonite's,
the shell is divided into
chambers. By regulating the
gas in these chambers, the
animal moves up or down in the water. It swims
backwards with its head pointing downwards.

ANCIENT ANCESTORS
This limestone is about 200 million years old.
It is packed with the remains of hundreds of
ammonites. These sea creatures had hard, coiled
shells, and are now extinct. Because the species
changed rapidly and lived in many areas of the
world, they can be used to determine the relative
ages of the rocks in which they occur. The nearest
modern equivalent to the ammonite is Nautilus,
which lives in the Pacific Ocean.

Ammonite remains

A GRAVEYARD FOR SNAILS
This piece of limestone contains the hard spiral
shells of marine gastropods (snails) from
about 120 million years ago. In places,
the white shell has dissolved, leaving an impression of the inside.

Impression of interior of shell

Gastropod shell

FOSSIL HUNTING
The abundance of
fossils at the seashore
made collecting a
popular pastime
during the 19th
century.

Garden snails

Rocks from space

EVERY YEAR about 19,000 meteorites each weighing over 100 g (4 oz) fall to the Earth. Most fall into the sea or on deserts, and only about five are recovered annually. Meteorites are natural objects that survive their fall from space. When they enter the Earth's atmosphere their surfaces melt and are swept away, but the interiors stay cold. As meteorites are slowed down by the atmosphere, the molten surface solidifies to form a dark, thin fusion crust.

PASAMONTE FIREBALL
Photographed by a ranch foreman in New Mexico, U.S.A., at 5 a.m., this fireball fell to Earth in March 1933. Meteorites are named after the places where they fall, this one being Pasamonte. The fireball had a low angled path some 800 km (500 miles) long. It broke up in the atmosphere, heralding the fall of dozens of meteoritic stones.

Fragment of meteorite

Dark, glassy fusion crust formed during passage through Earth's atmosphere

Grey interior consisting mainly of the minerals olivine and pyroxene

METALLIC METEORITE
The Cañon Diablo meteorite collided with the Earth about 20,000 years ago. Unlike Barwell, it is an iron meteorite. These are rarer than stony meteorites and consist of an iron-nickel alloy containing about 5-12 per cent nickel. They once formed parts of small asteroids (opposite) which broke up. The largest meteorite known is an iron, the Hoba, Namibia, which weighs about 60 tonnes. This cut piece of Cañon Diablo has been polished and partly etched with acid to reveal its internal structure.

EARTH'S CONTEMPORARY *above*
The Barwell meteorite fell at Barwell, Leicestershire, England, on Christmas Eve, 1965. The meteorite is 4,600 million years old and formed at the same time as the Earth but in a different part of the Solar System. Of every ten meteorites seen to fall, eight are "stones" like Barwell.

METAL AND STONE *below*
"Stony-irons" form a separate group of meteorites. The surface of this slice of the Thiel Mountains meteorite has been cut and polished to show bright metal enclosing stony material, the mineral olivine. It was found in Antarctica where meteorites have been on Earth for about 300,000 years and for much of this time have been encased in ice.

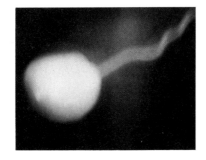

EXPLOSION CRATER
When the Cañon Diablo meteorite hit Arizona, U.S.A., about 15,000 tonnes of meteorite exploded. It created an enormous hole, Meteor Crater, about 1.2 km (0.75 mile) across and nearly 180 m (600 ft) deep. Only 30 tonnes of meteorite remained, scattered as small fragments across the surrounding countryside.

Metal

Stony part containing olivine

HALLEY'S COMET
Water-bearing meteorites may have come from comets, such as Halley's - here depicted in the Bayeux tapestry.

ASTEROID STRUCTURE
Many meteorites come from minor planets, the asteroids. They were never part of a single planet, but circle around the sun between the orbits of Mars and Jupiter. The largest asteroid, Ceres, is 1,020 km (632 miles) across, but most asteroids are less than 100 km (62 miles) in diameter. Their interiors consist of: a central core of metal, which is the source for some iron meteorites like Cañon Diablo; a core-mantle region which provides stony-iron meteorites like Thiel Mountains; and a crust which provides stony meteorites like Barwell.

Crust

Mantle

Core-mantle

Core

WATER-BEARERS
The Murchison meteorite fell in Australia in 1969. It contains carbon compounds and water from space. Material similar to this is believed to form the nucleus of a comet. The carbon compounds were formed by chemical reactions and not by a living organism. Such meteorites are rare - only about three falls in 100 are of this type.

Rocks from the Moon and Mars

Five meteorites found in Antarctica are known to have come from the Moon because they are like lunar highlands rocks collected by the Apollo missions. Eight other meteorites are thought to have come from Mars.

MARTIAN ORIGIN
The Nakhla stone fell in Egypt in 1911 and is reported to have killed a dog. This stone formed 1,300 million years ago, much more recently than most meteorites, and probably came from Mars.

LUNAR DISCOVERIES
The lunar meteorites are made of the same material as the lunar highlands boulder next to Apollo 17 astronaut, Jack Schmitt.

MOON ROCK
The Moon's surface is covered with soil made of minute rock and mineral fragments. It was formed by repeated bombardment of the surface by meteorites. Material like this on the surface of an asteroid was compacted to form many stony meteorites. Here, the light-coloured mineral is feldspar, and the darker mineral is pyroxene.

Petrological
microscope

Rock-forming minerals

Eight elements make up nearly 99 per cent of
the Earth's crust. These elements combine to form
naturally occurring minerals. Silicate minerals and
silica predominate in most common rocks except limestones. Igneous rocks form
the greatest part of the rocky interior of the earth, and specific rock-forming
mineral groups are characteristic of certain types of igneous rocks.

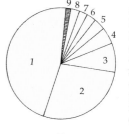

**COMPOSITION OF THE
EARTH'S CRUST**
In weight per cent
order, the elements are:
oxygen (1), silicon (2),
aluminium (3), iron (4),
calcium (5) sodium (6),
potassium (7), mag-
nesium (8), and all
other elements (9).

Minerals in granitic rocks

The minerals that form granitic and dioritic rocks include
feldspars, quartz, micas and amphiboles. Feldspars are
the most abundant of all minerals, and occur in nearly all
types of rock.

*Group of
black
prismatic
crystals with
calcite*

Single
hornblende
crystal

Quartz or
rock crystal

SILICA MINERALS
These include quartz, chalcedony (p. 52) and opal (p. 51).
Quartz is one of the most widely distributed minerals,
occuring in igneous, sedimentary and metamorphic
rocks. It is characteristic of granites,
gneisses and quartzites.

POTASSIC FELDSPARS
Orthoclase is found in many igneous
and metamorphic rocks,
while microcline (the
lower temperature
form of orthoclase)
is found in granite
pegmatites.

Green microcline
(or amazonstone)
crystal

Twinned crystals of
pink orthoclase

Hornblende, an
amphibole, common in
igneous rocks and in
metamorphic rocks such
as hornblende schists

Tremolite, an amphibole,
common in meta-
morphic rocks

THIN SECTION OF A GRANITIC ROCK
When a slice of diorite about 0.03 mm thick
is viewed under a petrological microscope
(above), it reveals coloured amphiboles,
plain grey to colourless quartz, and lined
grey plagioclase feldspar.

*Silvery, radiating,
needle-like crystals*

AMPHIBOLES
This group of minerals is widely
found in igneous and metamorphic
rocks. Amphiboles can be
distinguished from pyroxenes
(opposite) by the characteristic
angles between their cleavage
planes (p. 48).

Muscovite, an
aluminium-rich
mica, is abundant
in schists and gneisses

Silvery brown tabular crystals

Biotite, a dark, iron-
rich mica usually found in
igneous rocks, is also a common
constituent of schists and gneisses

MICAS
There are two main types of mica: dark
iron- and magnesium-rich mica, and white
aluminium-rich mica. All have perfect cleavage
(p. 48), splitting into thin flakes.

Minerals in basic rocks

The seven minerals shown here are all commonly found in basic rocks like basalts and gabbros.

Pink anorthite crystals, a plagioclase feldspar, with augite

Twinned albite crystals, a plagioclase feldspar, with calcite

OLIVINE

This silicate of iron and magnesium is typically found in silica-poor rocks such as basalts, gabbros and peridotites. It often forms as small grains or large, granular masses. Clear crystals are cut as gem peridots (p. 54).

Green olivine crystals

Volcanic bomb containing olivine, from Vesuvius (p. 18)

Single crystal of augite

Nepheline, a feldspathoid, with calcite

PLAGIOCLASE FELDSPARS *above*

This series of minerals contains varying proportions of sodium and calcium. Plagioclase feldspars are common constituents of igneous rocks.

FELDSPATHOIDS

As their name suggests, these minerals are related to feldspars, but they contain less silica and are typically formed in silica-poor volcanic lavas.

THIN SECTION OF A BASIC ROCK

A section of olivine basalt in polarized light reveals brightly coloured olivine, brown-yellow pyroxene, and minute lined, grey plagioclase feldspars.

Leucite crystal, a feldspathoid, on volcanic rock

Prismatic crystal of enstatite with biotite

Greenish-black prismatic crystals of augite, a pyroxene

PYROXENES

The most common pyroxenes are calcium, magnesium and iron silicates. Augite is a widely distributed pyroxene, and is found abundantly in igneous rocks such as gabbros and basalts. Less common is enstatite, which is found in gabbros, pyroxenites and some peridotites.

Other rock-forming minerals

There are two other important groups of rock-forming minerals - carbonates and clays.

Montmorillonite

CARBONATES

These are important constituents of sedimentary (limestones) or metamorphic (marble) rocks, also in ore-vein deposits. The most common is calcite, the main constituent of limestones.

Kaolinite (china clay) formed from partly decomposed orthoclase

Illite

CLAYS

An important part of the sedimentary rock sequence, clays form from the weathering and alteration of aluminous silicates. Clays include kaolinite, montmorillonite and illite.

Dolomite, a carbonate, found in some sedimentary deposits usually interbedded with limestones

Crystals

THROUGH THE AGES man has been fascinated by the intrinsic beauty of crystals. For centuries it was thought that rock crystal, a variety of quartz, was ice that had frozen so hard it would never thaw. The word crystal is derived from the Greek word *kryos* meaning icy cold. In fact, a crystal is a solid with a regular internal structure. Because of the arrangement of its atoms, a crystal may form smooth external surfaces called faces. Different crystals of the same mineral may develop the same faces but they may not necessarily be the same size or shape. Many crystals have important commercial uses, and some are cut as gemstones (p. 50).

Crystal collecting
in the Alps, c. 1870

Light reflecting on the crystal face

*Crystals orientated in
random growth directions*

Lines of striations formed as the crystal grew

Large twin crystal

Plane of intersection

Well-developed faces

SCULPTED "ICE"
Beautiful groups of natural crystals like this rock crystal look as if they have been artificially cut and polished. This specimen, found in Isère, France, is particularly well-formed consisting of a large twin crystal (opposite) and many simple crystals. The narrow ridges and furrows across some of its faces are called striations. These were formed when two different crystal faces attempted to develop at the same time.

Crystal symmetry

Crystals can be grouped into the seven systems shown below according to their symmetry. This is reflected in certain regular features of the crystal. For example, for every face there may be another on the opposite side of the crystal that is parallel to it and similar in shape and size. However, in most mineral specimens it may be difficult to determine the symmetry because crystals occur as aggregates and do not have well-developed faces.

SCIENTIFIC MEASUREMENT
A useful feature in identifying crystals is that the angle between corresponding faces of a particular mineral is always the same. Scientists measure this accurately using a contact goniometer.

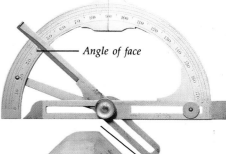

Angle of face

Angle between crystal faces being measured

TRICLINIC
Crystals in this system exhibit the least symmetry - as shown by this wedge-shaped axinite crystal from Brazil. Plagioclase feldspars (p. 43) are also triclinic minerals.

CUBIC
Metallic pyrite (p. 59) forms cube-shaped crystals but other cubic mineral forms include octahedra and tetrahedra. Garnet (p. 55) is also classified in this system. Crystals in this system exhibit the highest symmetry.

TETRAGONAL
Dark green idocrase crystals, like this Siberian specimen, are grouped with zircon (p. 54) and wulfenite (p. 9) in the tetragonal system.

ORTHORHOMBIC
Common ortho-rhombic minerals include baryte (from which we get barium for medicinal uses), olivine (p. 43) and topaz (p. 54).

RHOMBOHEDRAL (TRIGONAL)
Smaller secondary crystals have grown on this siderite crystal. Quartz (opposite), corundum (p. 51), tourmaline (p. 55) and calcite (pp. 22 and 48) belong to the same system.

MONOCLINIC
The most common crystal system includes gypsum (from which we make plaster of Paris, p. 21) azurite (p. 33) and orthoclase (p. 49).

HEXAGONAL
Beryl (p. 50), including this Colombian emerald variety, crystallizes in the hexagonal system as does apatite (p. 49) and ice. This does not prevent every snowflake having a unique appearance.

Snowflakes

Twinning

Crystals may grow in groups in cavities in mineral veins. Occasionally they develop in such a way that two (or sometimes more) individual crystals appear to intersect in a symmetrical manner. Related crystals like this are known as "twin crystals".

CONTACT TWINS
The mineral cerussite crystallizes in the orthorhombic system. This group of twin crystals was found in Namibia.

PENETRATION TWINS
Staurolite is also an orthorhombic mineral. In this cross-shaped Brazilian specimen one twin appears to penetrate into the other.

Twinned gypsum crystals form a distinctive arrow-shape from which they get their common name, "swallow-tail"

The growing crystal

No two crystals are exactly alike because the conditions in which they develop vary. They can only grow where there is sufficient space, and if this is restricted, distortions or unusual features may develop. Crystals range in size from microscopic to several metres long. The shape and size of a crystal or aggregate of crystals constitute its "habit".

Coral-like shape

WHITE CORAL
Aragonite, which was named after the Spanish province of Aragon, can sometimes have a "coralloid" habit. This term is used to describe minerals whose shape resembles corals.

Fine crystal "needles"

RADIATING NEEDLES
Very slender, elongated crystals with a needle-like appearance are described as having an "acicular" habit. In this scolecite specimen, grey acicular crystals radiate from the centre.

METALLIC "GRAPES"
Some chalcopyrite (p. 59) crystals grow outwards from a centre and such aggregates appear as rounded nodules. The habit is "botryoidal", a term strictly meaning like a bunch of grapes.

SPARKLING AGGREGATE *below right*
Hematite (p. 33) occurs in a number of different habits. When it forms lustrous, sparkling crystals it is said to have a "specular" habit, named from the Latin *speculum* meaning to reflect. The specimen shown consists of an aggregate of specular crystals.

CRYSTAL COLUMNS
"Prismatic" crystals are much longer in one direction than in the other two. This beryl crystal (p. 50) has six large rectangular prism faces and a flat hexagonal terminal face at each end.

Equant garnet crystals

Mica schist

SOFT STRANDS *left*
Crystals of tremolite, one of several minerals commonly known as asbestos, are soft and extremely pliable. Their habit is known as "fibrous" because the crystals resemble material fibres.

LAYERED SHEETS
Certain minerals, including mica (p. 42), divide into thin sheets (p. 48). They are said to be "micaceous" or, alternatively, "foliated" meaning leaf-like or "lamellar" meaning thin and platy.

EQUAL SIDES
Many minerals develop crystals which are essentially equal in all dimensions, and are then said to be "equant". This specimen of garnet (p. 55) in mica schist is a fine example.

DUAL FORM

Pyrite (p. 59) may crystallize as simple cubes and also as 12-faced solids called pentagonal dodecahedra. If the conditions change during growth, both forms may co-develop, resulting in a series of striations (p. 44) on the crystal faces.

Strongly striated, cubic faces

Sloping dodecahedral faces

Top of glistening pink calcite crystal group

Base of grey calcite crystal group

PARALLEL LINES

During crystal growth a series of crystals of the same type may develop growing in the same direction. This calcite aggregate shows a number of tapering pale pink and grey crystals in perfect parallel orientation.

SALT LAKE, CYPRUS

When salt lakes dry up, a thick crust of soluble salts is left.

Stepped faces

DOUBLE DECKER

Chalcopyrite (p. 59) and sphalerite (p. 57) crystals have similar structures. Here, tarnished, brassy-metallic chalcopyrite crystals have grown in parallel orientation on brownish-black sphalerite crystals.

Sphalerite crystals

Chalcopyrite crystals

STEPPED CRYSTALS

This specimen of halite (p. 21) contains numerous sand grains. It shows excessive growth in two directions along preferred axes, resulting in a stack of cubic crystals forming steps.

Sandy cubes

HOPPER GROWTH

The mineral halite (salt, p. 21) is cubic but crystals sometimes grow from solution faster along the cube edge than in the centre of the faces, resulting in the formation of "hopper crystals" that have stepped cavities in each face.

BRANCHING METAL

Where space is restricted, such as in confined spaces between two beds of rock, native copper (p. 56) and other minerals may grow in thin sheets. Its characteristic branch-like form is described as "dendritic".

"Branches" of copper

Outline of chlorite

PHANTOM GROWTH

The dark areas within this quartz crystal formed when a thin layer of chlorite coated the crystal at an earlier stage of its growth. As the crystal continued to grow, the chlorite became a ghost-like outline.

The properties of minerals

THE MAJORITY OF MINERALS have a regular crystal structure and a definite chemical composition. These determine the physical and chemical properties that are characteristic for each particular mineral, some having considerable scientific and industrial importance. By studying mineral properties such as cleavage, hardness and specific gravity, geologists can discover how the mineral was formed and use them, along with colour and habit (p. 46), to identify minerals.

Structure

Some chemically identical minerals exist in more than one structural state. The element carbon, for example, forms two minerals - diamond and graphite. The difference in their properties is caused by different arrangements of carbon atoms.

Carbon atom

Model of graphite structure

Model of diamond structure

Carbon atom

Model showing how one atom is bonded to four others

Diamonds

GRAPHITE
In graphite, a hexagonal mineral formed under high temperature conditions, each carbon atom is closely linked to three others in the same plane. The structure is built up of widely spaced layers which are only weakly bonded together. Graphite is one of the softest minerals (Mohs scale 1-2), and its loose bonding enables it to leave marks on paper, hence its use in pencils.

Graphite specimen

DIAMOND
In diamond (p. 50), a cubic mineral formed under high pressure conditions, each carbon atom is strongly bonded to four others to form a rigid compact structure. This makes diamond extremely hard (Mohs scale 10). Because of this, it is used as an industrial cutting tool.

Cleavage

When crystals break, some have a tendency to split along well-defined cleavage planes. These are caused by the orderly arrangement of the atoms in the crystal.

Thin layers

THIN SHEETS
Stibnite, an ore of antimony, shows a perfect sheet-like cleavage due to weak structural bonding between chains of antimony and sulphur atoms.

LEAD STEPS
Galena, the main ore of lead (p. 57), has a perfect cubic cleavage, due to the internal arrangement of lead and sulphur atoms, so that a broken crystal face consists of many small cubic cleavage steps.

Steps

PERFECT BREAK
Baryte crystals (p. 45) show an intersecting, perfect cleavage. If this crystal was broken, it would split along these planes of cleavage.

Thin lines show cleavage planes

Smaller crystal growing with larger crystal

PERFECT RHOMB
Any piece of calcite has such a well-developed rhombohedral cleavage that a break in any other direction is virtually impossible.

FRACTURE
Quartz crystals break with a glassy, conchoidal (shell-like) fracture rather than cleaving along any particular plane.

Rounded, conchoidal edges

Hardness

The bonds holding atoms together dictate a mineral's hardness. In 1812, the Austrian mineralogist Friedrich Mohs devised a scale of hardness that is still in use today. He selected ten minerals as standards and arranged them so that any mineral on the scale would scratch only those below it. Everyday objects can be used to test where a mineral fits into the scale. A fingernail has a hardness of 2.5, and a penknife is 5.5. Minerals of six and above will scratch glass, while glass will itself scratch apatite and other minerals below it.

GRAPH SHOWING RELATIVE HARDNESS
The intervals between the minerals in Mohs' scale are irregular. Diamond is about 40 times harder than talc, while corundum is only nine times as hard.

1	2	3	4	5	6	7	8	9	10
Talc	Gypsum	Calcite	Fluorite	Apatite	Orthoclase	Quartz	Topaz	Corundum	Diamond

Magnetism

Only two common minerals, magnetite and pyrrhotine (both iron compounds), are strongly magnetic. Some specimens of magnetite called "lodestones" were used as an early form of compass.

NATURAL MAGNET
Magnetite is permanently magnetized and will attract iron filings and other metallic objects such as paper clips.

Clusters of iron filings

Optical properties

As light passes through minerals, a variety of optical effects is produced due to the interaction of light with atoms in the structure.

DOUBLE IMAGE
Light travelling through a calcite rhomb is split into two rays, making a single daisy stalk appear to the eye as two.

FLUORESCING AUTUNITE
When viewed under ultraviolet light, certain minerals fluoresce.

Specific gravity

This property relates a mineral's chemical composition to its crystal structure. It is defined as the ratio of the weight of a substance to that of an equal volume of water. Determining the specific gravity may aid identification.

SIZE v. WEIGHT
The nature of the atoms and internal atomic arrangement of a mineral determines its specific gravity. These three mineral specimens all weigh the same, but because the atoms in quartz and galena are heavier or more closely packed together than those in mica, the quartz and galena specimens are much smaller.

Mica

Quartz

Galena

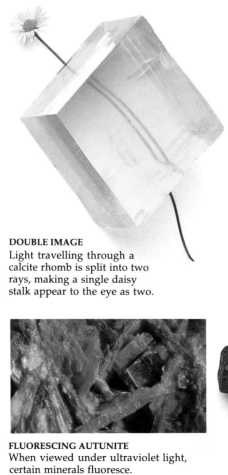

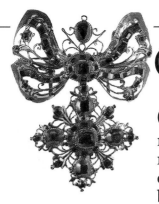

Gemstones

GEMSTONES are naturally occurring minerals that are exceptional for their beauty and rarity, and are sufficiently resilient to survive everyday wear when used to decorate jewellery and artifacts. Diamond, emerald, ruby, sapphire and opal all fit this description. Light reflects and refracts with the minerals to produce the intense colours of ruby and emerald, and the "fire" of diamond. Colour, fire and lustre are commonly revealed only by skilled cutting and polishing (p. 60). Gems are commonly weighed by the carat, equal to one fifth of a gram, and not to be confused with the carat used to describe the quality of gold (p. 59).

Diamond

Diamond is named from the Greek word *adamas* meaning unconquerable, and is the hardest of all known minerals (p. 49). It is famed for its lasting fiery brilliance. The quality of a gem diamond is measured by its colour, its clarity, the quality of its cut and its carat weight - popularly known as "the four C's".

Kimberley mine, South Africa

TREASURES IN GRAVEL
Before 1870 diamonds were found only as crystals or fragments in river gravels, mainly in India or Brazil. In the late 1800s, the discovery first of diamond-bearing gravels and then kimberlite made South Africa the leading supplier.

Diamond crystal
Kimberlite

DIAMONDS IN ROCK
Kimberlite is the source rock for most diamonds. It is named after Kimberley in South Africa where it occurs in a volcanic pipe that has its roots between 100 and 200 miles deep in the Earth's crust.

Beryl

The most important gem varieties - emerald and aquamarine - have been exploited for centuries: Egyptian emerald mines date back to 1650 BC. Beautifully formed, hexagonal beryl crystals may be found in pegmatites and schists in Brazil, U.S.S.R., and many other countries.

Cut emerald

EMERALDS
The finest emeralds, such as those in the British Crown Jewels, come from Colombia where they occur in veins with calcite and pyrite. Flawless emeralds are very rare and most crystals contain small blemishes or mineral inclusions. Superficially, these may seem to detract from a stone, but in fact they may be crucial in proving its natural origin.

ROMAN BERYL JEWELLERY
The earrings and necklaces contain cut emeralds.

Aquamarine

Greenish heliodor

Yellow heliodor

Pink morganite

THE ASSORTED COLOURS OF BERYL
Pure beryl is colourless. The gems' colours are due to impurities such as manganese which produces the pink of morganites. Greenish-blue aquamarine crystals are often heat-treated to produce a more intense blue colour.

MULTI-COLOURED DIAMONDS
Diamond ranges from colourless through yellow and brown to pink, green and blue. Red diamond is very rare. To show the stones to best advantage diamond cutters have, for centuries, fashioned table and rose-cut stones and, more recently, brilliant cuts which display the inherent fire and lustre (p. 60).

KOH-I-NOOR DIAMOND
This famous Indian diamond, here worn by Queen Mary of England, was presented to Queen Victoria in 1850.

Corundum

The beauty of ruby and sapphire lies in the richness and intensity of their colours. Both are varieties of the mineral corundum, which is colourless when pure. Tiny quantities of chromium give rise to the red of ruby, and iron and titanium are responsible for the blues, yellows and greens of sapphire.

STAR SAPPHIRE
Some stones contain very fine needle-like crystals orientated in three directions. Suitable cutting will give star rubies or star sapphires.

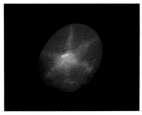

SAPPHIRE CRYSTAL
While ruby tends to form in flat crystals, sapphires are generally barrel-shaped or pyramidal. They often feature zones of blue to yellow colour that are important in choosing which crystals to cut.

RIVER JEWELS
Most sapphires and rubies are extracted from gem-rich gravels. The gem minerals are usually harder and more resistant to chemical weathering than their parent rocks and become concentrated in river beds.

GEMSTONES IN JEWELLERY
The oldest jewellery comes from ceremonial burials 20,000 years ago. Here, rubies, emeralds and diamonds decorate a late-16th-century enamelled, gold pendant.

RUBY CRYSTAL
Known as the Edwardes Ruby, this crystal is of exceptional quality, weighing 162 carats. It is almost certainly from the famous gem deposits of Mogok, Burma.

Cut ruby

GEM SOURCES
Australia is the most prolific source of blue and yellow sapphires, while rubies are mined in Burma, Thailand and central Africa. The rich gem gravels of Sri Lanka have for at least 2,000 years supplied exceptional blue and pink sapphires.

Blue sapphire

Pink sapphire

Colourless sapphire

Clear sapphire

Mauve sapphire

Yellow sapphire

Opal

The name opal probably derives from the Sanskrit word *upala*, meaning precious stone. However, the opals used by the Romans in their jewellery did not come from India, but from Czechoslovakia. In the 16th century, opal was brought to Europe from Central America and only after 1870 did Australia assume dominance in the world opal market.

OPAL MINING IN AUSTRALIA
Aside from its use in jewellery, opal mined today is also used in the manufacture of abrasives and insulation products.

COLOUR VARIATIONS IN OPAL
The beautiful blue, green, yellow and red iridescence in precious opal is caused by the reflection and scattering of light from minute silica spheres within the mineral. This is different from the background or "body" colour, which may be clear as in water opal, milky as in white opal or either grey or black as in the most precious form, black opal.

Iridescent black opals

White opal

Milky opal

OPAL'S ROCKY ORIGINS
Most opal forms over long periods of time in sedimentary rocks, as in this sample from Australia. However, in Mexico and Czechoslovakia opal forms in gas cavities in volcanic rocks. It is often cut as cabochons (p. 60), but the veins in sedimentary rocks are commonly thin and slices of these may be glued onto onyx or glass to form doublets. Such stones may be further "enhanced" with a cap of clear quartz to form a triplet.

FIRE OPAL
The finest fire opal comes from Mexico and Turkey and is generally cut as faceted stones. It is valued as much for its intensity of colour as for its iridescence.

Decorative stones

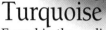

TURQUOISE, agate, lapis lazuli and jade are all gems made up of many crystals. They are valued mainly for their colour, either evenly distributed as in fine turquoise, or patterned as in an agate cameo. The toughness of jade and agate makes them ideal for delicate carving, while the softer turquoise is used for "protected" settings, such as pendants or inlay. Lapis lazuli is variable in quality and fine carving is only possible in high quality material.

Chalcedony

Chrysoprase cabochon

Cornelian, onyx, agate and chrysoprase are all forms of chalcedony. Pure chalcedony is translucent grey or white and consists of thin layers of tiny quartz fibres. Obviously banded chalcedony is called agate, and the different colours and patterns are caused by impurities.

ANCIENT FAVOURITE
Apple-green chrysoprase has been used in jewellery since pre-Roman times, commonly as cameos or intaglios in rings and pendants.

Vein of turquoise

Lapis lazuli

Blue lapis lazuli is composed mainly of the minerals lazurite and sodalite with smaller amounts of white calcite and specks of brassy coloured pyrite.

PUREST SAMPLES
The best lapis lazuli is mined in Badakhshan, Afghanistan, where it occurs in lenses and veins in white marble.

Turquoise

Found in the earliest jewellery, turquoise is so universally recognized that "turquoise-blue" is an accepted term for a pale greenish-blue. Its colour is largely due to copper and traces of iron. The more iron that is present, the greener (and less valuable) the turquoise.

ANCIENT LAPIS JEWELLERY
For centuries lapis has been fashioned into beads or carvings. It has been known for over 6,000 years and is named from the Persian word _Lazhward_, meaning blue.

CUT TURQUOISE
The finest sky-blue turquoise occurs in Nishapur, Iran, where it has been mined for about 3,000 years. Another ancient source, known to the Aztecs, is the southwestern United States. Nowadays, this supplies most of the world's turquoise.

MESOPOTAMIAN MOSAIC
Lapis was used to decorate the wooden box known as the "Standard of Ur", c. 2,500 BC.

TURQUOISE ORNAMENTS
This artefact may be of Persian origin. The double-headed serpent (top) is an Aztec necklace. It was sent to Cortez by Montezuma during the 15-16th century.

EGYPTIAN AMULET
Many fine pieces of early Egyptian craftsmanship have been recovered from the tombs of the Kings.

TRUE BLUE _left_
The vivid blue of this lapis slice is caused by small amounts of sulphur, and has been imitated in glass, and even synthetic lapis.

AGATE
Fine-grained, banded agates form in cavities in volcanic rocks. The most prolific sources of good agate are in Brazil and Uruguay.

POLISHED AGATE
The beautiful patterns shown in polished agate slices were caused when microscopic crystals formed in bands and coloured deposits as hot, silica-rich solutions filtered through cavities in porous rocks.

CARVED PORTRAIT
Bloodstone cameos were popular in Roman times.

Crystals

Deep-coloured band

STONE LANDSCAPE
The pattern in moss agate or mocha stone is shown to advantage in this delicate cabochon.

ORNAMENTAL KNIFE
Cornelian is red chalcedony and has been used extensively in decorative jewellery and inlay work throughout history. Here, it has been fashioned into a knife.

Jade
Originally named from the Spanish *piedra de hijada* used to describe the green stone carved by the Indians in Central America, jade actually refers to two different substances – jadeite and nephrite.

TUTANKHAMUN'S MASK
Lapis, cornelian, obsidian and quartz are inlaid in gold along with assorted coloured glass.

RARE JADE
Jadeite may be white orange, brown or, rarely, lilac, but the most prized is "imperial jade", a translucent emerald green variety.

MOGUL DAGGER
Pale green and grey nephrite was a favourite material of the Mogul craftsmen who fashioned dagger handles, bowls and personal jewellery, often inlaid with rubies and other gems.

CHINESE ART
The toughness of jade was known to the Chinese more than 2,000 years ago and this was exploited in their delicate carvings. These were executed in nephrite until Burmese jadeite became available, c. 1750.

NEPHRITE BOULDERS
Nephrite is more common than jadeite and is generally green, grey or creamy white. Much jade occurs as waterworn boulders and this example of nephrite from New Zealand is typical.

Lesser-known gems

In addition to the well-known gemstones such as diamond, ruby, sapphire, emerald and opal, many other minerals have been used for human adornment. Beautiful features like the lustre and fire of zircon and demantoid garnet, and the multicoloured hues of the tourmaline family have attracted attention. There is space here only to glimpse some examples of the stones more frequently seen in jewellery, but the range of colour even in these species is extensive.

Multicoloured topaz

Blue topaz

Yellow topaz

TOPAZ
Occuring chiefly in granites and pegmatites, some gem-quality topaz crystals are very large, weighing many kilograms. The largest stones are colourless or pale blue but the most valuable in terms of price per carat are golden-yellow - "imperial topaz" - or pink, both of which are found in Brazil. Pakistan is the only other source of pink topaz but yellow topaz is slightly more common, while colourless topaz is found worldwide.

Blue spinel

Pink spinel

Mauve spinel

Cut spinel

TOPAZ BROOCH
Brown topaz was commonly used in 18th- and 19th-century jewellery. The rarer pink stones were synthetically produced by heating yellow topaz.

SPINEL
Red spinels are very similar to rubies. They were once called balas rubies, probably after Balascia, now Badakhshan in Afghanistan, their supposed source. Fine red spinels also come from Burma and from Sri Lanka where there is also a range of pink, lilac, blue and bluish-green stones.

BLACK PRINCE'S RUBY
This famous spinel is the central stone in the British Imperial State Crown.

PERIDOT
This is the transparent gem variety of olivine (p. 43), a mineral common in basaltic lavas and some deep-seated igneous rocks. The proportion of iron in the mineral determines the shade of colour - the more valuable golden-green and deep-green stones containing less iron than those with a brownish tinge. Peridot is softer than quartz with a distinctive oily lustre, and has been used in jewellery since classical times. The original source was the island of Zebirget in the Red Sea, but fine material has since come from Burma, Norway and Arizona, U.S.A.

Vermilion zircon

Pink zircon

Green zircon

Yellow zircon

Blue zircon

ZIRCON
Named from the Arabic word *zargoon* meaning vermilion or golden coloured, stones of these colours, in addition to green and brown varieties, have been used in Indian jewellery for centuries. When transparent stones are cut and polished they display a lustre and fire similar to diamond, but they are softer and chip more easily.

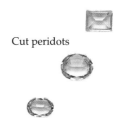

Cut peridots

GARNET

Garnet is a group name for a diverse set of gems which includes almandine and pyrope (red and purplish-red), spessartine (orange-red), grossular (orange, green or colourless) and demantoid (green). Fine demantoid has a colour rivalling that of emerald and a fire exceeding that of diamond. Its beauty and rarity command a high price. Almandine and pyrope cabochons, faceted stones and carvings have been popular for more than 2,000 years. The best spessartines and orange grossulars come from Brazil and Sri Lanka, and the best demantoids from the Ural mountains.

GARNET EARRINGS
Rose-cut stones (p. 60) make attractive jewellery when set in gold, as shown by these 18th-century earrings.

Rose-cut stone

Gold

Almandine   Hessonite   Pyrope   Demantoid

Grossular garnets

Demantoid garnets

19th-century amethyst necklace

Cut amethyst

GREEK DIADEM
This section of an enamelled, Hellenistic diadem dates from the 2nd century, and is inlaid with garnets. Its design is common to many contemporary Greek artifacts.

AMETHYST
Purple amethyst is a variety of quartz (p. 44). Colourless, transparent rock crystal is the purest form of quartz, and the colours of amethyst, citrine (yellow quartz) and rose quartz are caused by iron or titanium impurities. The finest crystalline amethyst occurs in gas cavities (geodes) in volcanic rocks in India, Uruguay and Brazil.

TOURMALINE
Tourmaline shows the greatest range in colour of any gemstone, and some single crystals are multicoloured. The crystal forms and the electrical properties are different at each end of a crystal and this polarity is sometimes reflected in colour differences, especially pink and green. Carvings and cut stones may show this variation to advantage. The best gem-quality tourmaline crystals come from pegmatites. Certain mines in California, U.S.A., are famed for pink and green crystals, and other fine material is found in the Ural mountains, Brazil and Madagascar.

Pink tourmaline   Brown tourmaline   Mauve-grey tourmaline   "Watermelon" tourmaline

Blue tourmaline

Green tourmaline

Yellowish-green tourmaline

Graduating colour tourmaline

BYZANTINE RELIC, c. 955
Many Byzantine artifacts were made of gold and decorated with precious stones.

Ore minerals and metals

THE ORE MINERALS are the source of most useful metals. After mining, quarrying or dredging, the ores are concentrated by crushing and separating processes, before being refined and smelted to produce metal. Even before 5,000 BC, copper was used to make beads and pins. However, it was the Mesopotamians who first began large-scale smelting and casting. Then, around 3,000 BC, tin was added to copper to produce the harder metal, bronze. Still more important was the production of iron which was fairly widespread by 500 BC. Iron is harder than bronze, and iron ores are much more widely available.

Bronze ritual food vessel from China, c. 10th century BC

Bauxite, aluminium ore (p. 13)

LIGHTWEIGHT ALUMINIUM
Aluminium is a good electrical conductor, light in weight and resistant to corrosion. It is used in power transmission lines, building and construction, cars and consumer goods, such as washing machines and saucepans.

Aluminium kitchen foil

Stacks of aluminium ingots

Hematite, iron ore

Iron mining, c. 1580

TOUGH IRON
Hematite, the most important iron ore, commonly occurs as "kidney ore" - so-called because of its shape. Iron is tough and hard, yet easy to work and can be cast, forged, machined, rolled and alloyed. It is used extensively in the construction industries. Steel and many household items are manufactured from iron.

Steel screw

Rutile, titanium ore

STRONG TITANIUM
Rutile, together with ilmenite, are the principal ores of titanium. Usually found in igneous or metamorphic rocks, these two minerals are concentrated in the weathering process and form deposits with other minerals, many of which are extracted as by-products. Because of its light weight and great strength, titanium is widely used in the aircraft industry, both in frames and engines.

Airliner partially constructed from titanium

COLOURFUL COPPER
Brassy yellow chalcopyrite and bluish-purple bornite are common copper ores. Massive ores are generally found in isolated deposits which are uneconomic to work, and most copper now comes from large, low-grade deposits. Because it is a good conductor, copper is used in the electricity industry, and its malleability makes it suitable for household water pipes. It is used in alloys with zinc (brass) and with tin (bronze).

Chalcopyrite, copper ore

Bornite, copper ore

Copper plumbing joint

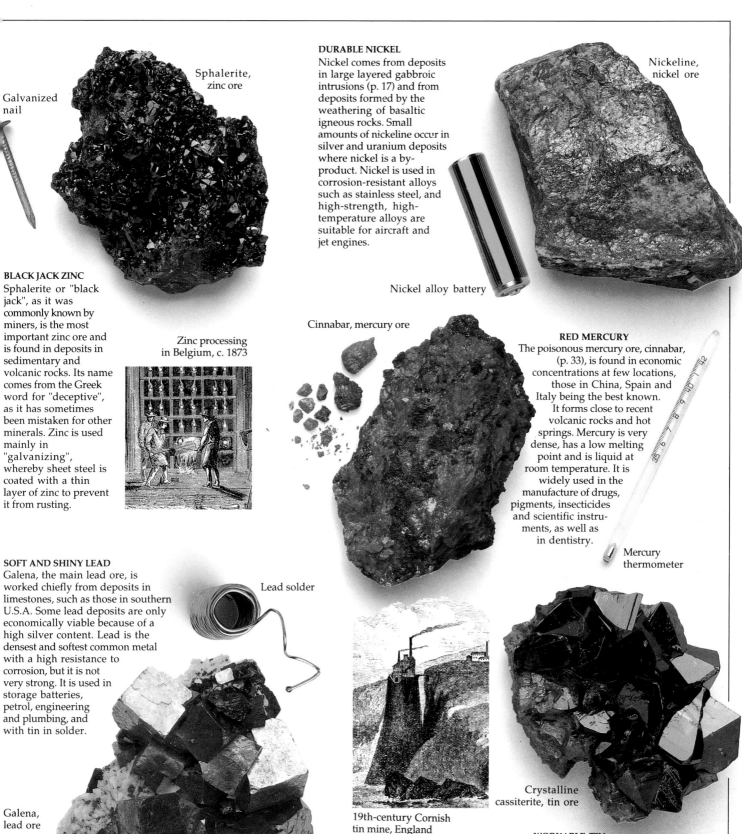

Galvanized nail

Sphalerite, zinc ore

DURABLE NICKEL

Nickel comes from deposits in large layered gabbroic intrusions (p. 17) and from deposits formed by the weathering of basaltic igneous rocks. Small amounts of nickeline occur in silver and uranium deposits where nickel is a by-product. Nickel is used in corrosion-resistant alloys such as stainless steel, and high-strength, high-temperature alloys are suitable for aircraft and jet engines.

Nickeline, nickel ore

Nickel alloy battery

BLACK JACK ZINC

Sphalerite or "black jack", as it was commonly known by miners, is the most important zinc ore and is found in deposits in sedimentary and volcanic rocks. Its name comes from the Greek word for "deceptive", as it has sometimes been mistaken for other minerals. Zinc is used mainly in "galvanizing", whereby sheet steel is coated with a thin layer of zinc to prevent it from rusting.

Zinc processing in Belgium, c. 1873

Cinnabar, mercury ore

RED MERCURY

The poisonous mercury ore, cinnabar, (p. 33), is found in economic concentrations at few locations, those in China, Spain and Italy being the best known. It forms close to recent volcanic rocks and hot springs. Mercury is very dense, has a low melting point and is liquid at room temperature. It is widely used in the manufacture of drugs, pigments, insecticides and scientific instruments, as well as in dentistry.

Mercury thermometer

SOFT AND SHINY LEAD

Galena, the main lead ore, is worked chiefly from deposits in limestones, such as those in southern U.S.A. Some lead deposits are only economically viable because of a high silver content. Lead is the densest and softest common metal with a high resistance to corrosion, but it is not very strong. It is used in storage batteries, petrol, engineering and plumbing, and with tin in solder.

Lead solder

Galena, lead ore

19th-century Cornish tin mine, England

Crystalline cassiterite, tin ore

WORKABLE TIN

The tin ore cassiterite is hard, heavy and resistant to abrasion. Crystalline forms, like this Bolivian specimen, are comparatively rare. The modern uses of tin are based on its low melting point, resistance to corrosion, malleability, lack of toxicity and high electrical conductivity. It is used in solder and tinplate, although aluminium is now more widely used for canning. Pewter is an alloy with roughly 75% tin and 25% lead.

Tin can

Precious metals

GOLD AND SILVER were among the earliest metals discovered and were valued for their beauty and comparative rarity. Both were used in coins and bars that were visible items of wealth and the principal means of exchange, as well as to make jewellery and other artifacts. Platinum was first reported from Colombia in the mid-18th century but was not widely used in jewellery and coinage until this century.

Platinum

Currently more valuable even than gold, platinum's major industrial use is in oil refining and in reducing pollution from car exhausts.

SPERRYLITE CRYSTAL
Platinum is found in a variety of minerals, one of which is sperrylite. This well-formed crystal was found in the Transvaal, South Africa around 1924. It is the world's largest known crystal of this species.

PLATINUM GRAINS
Most platinum minerals occur as very small grains in nickel deposits. However, platinum-bearing grains are also commonly recovered from gold workings. These grains are from Rio Pinto, Colombia.

RUSSIAN COINS
Platinum has been used as coinage in several countries. During the reign of Nicholas I, the Russians minted platinum coins worth three roubles.

PLATINUM NUGGET
Very rarely, large nuggets of platinum are found. This one, from Nijni-Tagilsk in the Urals, weighs 1.1 kg (2.3 lb) - impressive, but less than the largest ever recorded, which weighed 9.7 kg (22 lb).

Silver

Less valuable than either gold or platinum, one of silver's main disadvantages is that it tarnishes easily. Both sterling and plated silver are made into jewellery and ornaments, and silver is also used in the photographic industry.

MEXICAN ORE-CRUSHER
Early methods of crushing silver ores were primitive but effective.

DELICATE SILVER WIRES
Silver is now mostly extracted as a by-product from the mining of copper and lead-zinc deposits. In the last century, it was usually mined as native metal. Particularly famous are silver "wires" from the Kongsberg mines in Norway.

CELTIC BROOCH
The Celts fashioned many intricate pieces of jewellery in silver.

SILVER BRANCHES
Occasionally, as in this specimen from Copiapo, Chile, silver occurs in delicate, branch-like "dendritic" forms (p. 47).

RELIGIOUS BELL
One of a pair, this silver Torah bell was made in Italy in the early 18th century and was used in Jewish ceremonies.

Gold

Today, this familiar yellow metal is important in jewellery, dentistry and the electronics industry, yet more than half the gold so laboriously mined returns to the earth - buried in bank vaults for investment purposes!

SOUTH AFRICAN MINE
Traditional gold mining methods were labour intensive, c. 1900.

THE GREAT GOLD RUSH
During the 19th century, the discovery of gold in both California, U.S.A., and Australia, fired the imagination of multitudes of prospectors who began panning in earnest.

Crystalline chalcopyrite

FOOL'S GOLD
Novices sometimes mistake either chalcopyrite or pyrite for gold because of their brassy colour, hence the term "fool's gold". Chalcopyrite, the main ore of copper, is greenish-yellow compared to gold, and is more brittle and harder, although not as hard as pyrite.

Massive chalcopyrite

VEIN GOLD
Gold may occur in quartz veins and sometimes forms rich encrustations. The gold is extracted by crushing the ore and obtaining a concentrate, which is then smelted.

PYRITE
Pyrite generally forms cubic crystals and, on a fresh surface, is closer in colour to "white gold" or electrum, an alloy of gold and silver, than to pure gold. However, pyrite is much harder than gold.

Tutankhamun's collar

GOLD GRAINS
Gold is also produced from the rounded grains which occur in some gravel and sand deposits. These deposits are worked either by panning or larger-scale dredging. The gold particles are separated out before smelting.

Crystalline pyrite

Massive pyrite

EGYPTIAN CRAFT
The ancient Egyptians were one of the earliest civilizations to master the art of goldsmithing. They used solid, beaten gold. Nowadays, copper and silver are often added to gold to make it harder. The gold content is then measured in carats.

Cutting and polishing stones

THE EARLIEST METHOD of fashioning stones was to rub one against another to produce a smooth surface which could then be engraved. Much later, professional craftsmen (lapidaries) became skilled at cutting precious stones to obtain the best optical effect and to maximize the size of the cut stone. In recent years, amateur lapidaries have shaped rounded "pebbles" of various minerals by reverting to the process of rubbing stones together, using a rotating drum.

Grinding and polishing agates in a German workshop, c. 1800

Cutting gems

When mined, many gemstones look dull (p. 50). To produce a desirable, sparkling gem, the lapidary must cut and polish it to enhance its natural qualities, bearing in mind the position of any flaws.

THE HARDEST CUT
Rough diamonds are marked with indian ink before cutting.

POPULAR CUTS
The first gemstones were cut into relatively simple shapes, such as the table cut, and cabochon cut. Later lapidaries experimented with more complex faceted cuts, such as the step cut for coloured stones, and the brilliant for diamond and other colourless stones.

Table cut

Cabochon

Rose cut

Emerald or step cut

Pear brilliant

Round brilliant

Hollow drum

Belt driven by motor

Lid of drum

Rollers

TUMBLING
A tumbling machine consists of an electrically driven hollow drum mounted on rollers. Mineral fragments are tumbled in the drum with coarse grit and water for about a week. This is repeated with finer grits until the pebbles are rounded and polished.

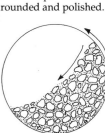

TUMBLING ACTION
As the drum rotates, pebbles are smoothed and rounded by the grit and each other.

Water added with grits

Rough mineral pieces ready for tumbling

GRITS AND POLISHES
Various grinding grits are used in sequence from the coarsest to the finest, followed by a polishing powder.

Coarse grinding grit used in first tumbling

Fine grinding grit used for second tumbling

Cerium oxide, very fine polishing powder, used finally to make pebbles smooth and sparkling

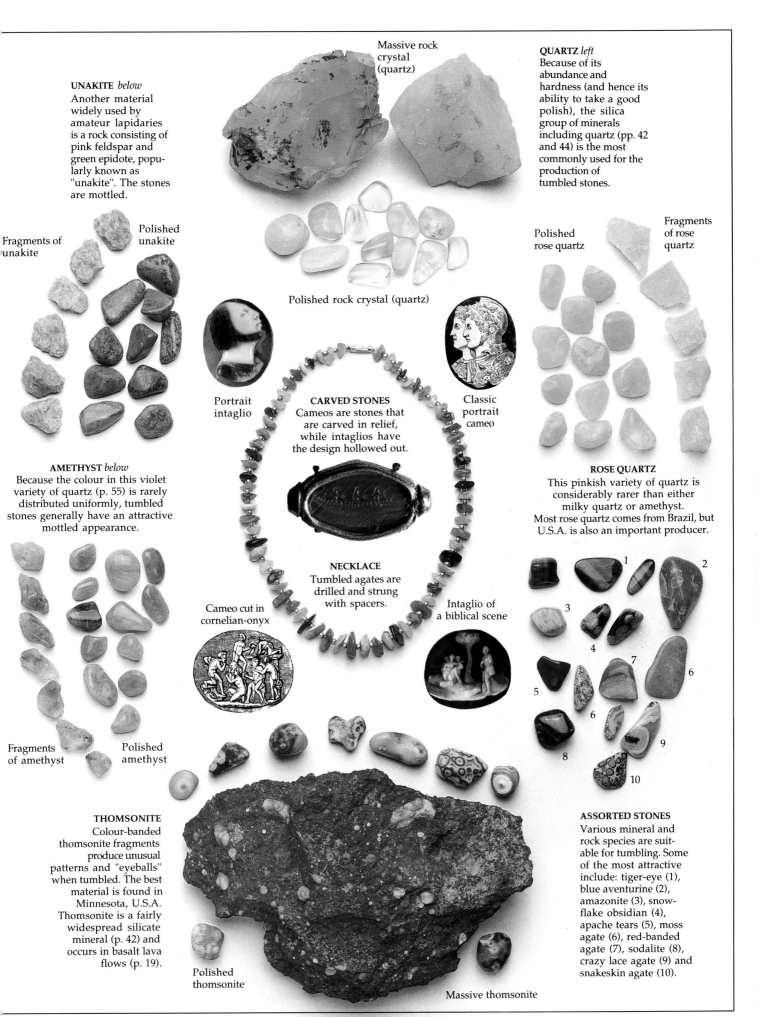

Massive rock crystal (quartz)

UNAKITE *below*
Another material widely used by amateur lapidaries is a rock consisting of pink feldspar and green epidote, popularly known as "unakite". The stones are mottled.

Polished unakite

Fragments of unakite

QUARTZ *left*
Because of its abundance and hardness (and hence its ability to take a good polish), the silica group of minerals including quartz (pp. 42 and 44) is the most commonly used for the production of tumbled stones.

Polished rock crystal (quartz)

Polished rose quartz

Fragments of rose quartz

Portrait intaglio

CARVED STONES
Cameos are stones that are carved in relief, while intaglios have the design hollowed out.

Classic portrait cameo

ROSE QUARTZ
This pinkish variety of quartz is considerably rarer than either milky quartz or amethyst. Most rose quartz comes from Brazil, but U.S.A. is also an important producer.

AMETHYST *below*
Because the colour in this violet variety of quartz (p. 55) is rarely distributed uniformly, tumbled stones generally have an attractive mottled appearance.

Cameo cut in cornelian-onyx

NECKLACE
Tumbled agates are drilled and strung with spacers.

Intaglio of a biblical scene

Fragments of amethyst

Polished amethyst

THOMSONITE
Colour-banded thomsonite fragments produce unusual patterns and "eyeballs" when tumbled. The best material is found in Minnesota, U.S.A. Thomsonite is a fairly widespread silicate mineral (p. 42) and occurs in basalt lava flows (p. 19).

Polished thomsonite

Massive thomsonite

ASSORTED STONES
Various mineral and rock species are suitable for tumbling. Some of the most attractive include: tiger-eye (1), blue aventurine (2), amazonite (3), snowflake obsidian (4), apache tears (5), moss agate (6), red-banded agate (7), sodalite (8), crazy lace agate (9) and snakeskin agate (10).

Collecting rocks and minerals

THE COLLECTING OF MINERAL and rock specimens and the recording of finds is a rewarding and popular pastime. As a hobby, it is in a tradition that dates back to the amateur geologists of the 19th century, many of whom amassed impressive collections.

COLLECTING TOOLS
The basic equipment required is a geological hammer, weighing between 0.5 and 1 kg (1 and 2 lb), and a range of chisels. Geological hammers usually have a square head and a chisel edge used for splitting rocks. They are specially tempered for the job; other types of hammer should not be used because they are more likely to splinter.

Club hammer for use with chisels

Geologist's hammer (0.5 kg/1 lb)

CAREFUL PLANNING
All field work and collecting trips should be planned in advance with reference to geological guide books and maps. Permission must be obtained to visit any area or site on private land. If you are collecting alone, make sure someone knows your intended route and destination. Always carry a compass to help with direction-finding and include a compass-bearing reference in your field notes.

Wide-ended chisel

Sharp, pointed chisel

Geologist's trimming hammer

FIELD WORK
During the 19th century, geologists working in the field developed the techniques of collecting and mapping rocks.

Map

Compass

Guide book

Safety helmet

PROTECTIVE CLOTHING
Great care must be taken when hammering rocks to prevent injury from flying rock and metal splinters. Wear protective goggles, a safety helmet, gloves, stout shoes or boots, and strong, waterproof clothing.

Strong gloves

Protective goggles

When rock-collecting, there are certain rules you should follow at all times: always obey the Country Code, ask permission before entering private land, avoid disturbing wildlife, wear suitable clothing, use proper equipment, and avoid creating hazards for others.

Notebook

Pencil

Pen

IDENTIFICATION
Specimens may be examined in the field with a x10 magnification hand lens. Indoors, a binocular microscope will reveal finer details.

RECORDING A FIND
The exact locality and details of a find should be recorded in a notebook, and the specimen carefully numbered using a pen or sticky tape. A photograph or sketch of the specimen before collection will provide a permanent field record.

Camera to record site or location of find - when taking photographs try to give some indication of scale

Spatulas for fine work, such as cutting around fossils

Surgical knife for fine preparatory work on fossils

Palette knife for excavating small crystals from soft fossils or minerals

Muslin bag

Newspaper

Plastic tube

TRANSPORTING SPECIMENS
Each specimen should be individually wrapped in newspaper or other protective material to prevent chipping or scratching. Crystal groups are usually very fragile and should be packed in tubes or boxes with suitable wrapping and carried in special collecting bags.

Bubble wrap

Sealable plastic bag

TOOLS FOR FINE WORK
Surplus rock can be removed from a specimen by washing in water and scrubbing lightly with a soft brush. Soft, friable rock, such as clay, may be dug with a trowel, then sieved for small crystals or rock fragments.

CURATING THE COLLECTION
To avoid damage to specimens, they should be stored in individual trays or boxes within a cabinet of shallow drawers. Some minerals deteriorate rapidly in damp conditions, at high temperatures or under the effects of light, so the needs of each one must be considered when organizing the collection.

Trowel for digging soft rocks

Sieve for sorting material

Paint brushes for cleaning specimens

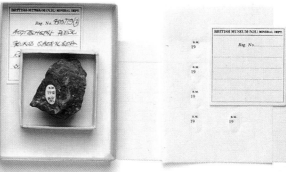

Cardboard boxes for storing specimens

Labels for documenting specimens

Did you know?

AMAZING FACTS

After astronauts returned from the Moon, scientists discovered that the most common type of rock on the Moon is a type of basalt that is also found on Earth.

Spider preserved in amber

The amber we find today formed when resin dripped from trees millions of years ago and then hardened. Sometimes, insects were trapped in the sticky resin before it set and were preserved to this day.

The deeper down inside the Earth a tunnel goes, the hotter it becomes. The deepest gold mines in South Africa have to be cooled down artificially so that people are able to work in them.

Devil's Tower, Wyoming

Devil's Tower, in Wyoming, USA, is a huge rock pillar made from lava that hardened inside the vent of a volcano. Over thousands of years, the softer rock of the volcano itself has worn away.

More than 75% of the Earth's crust is made of silicates, minerals composed of silicon, oxygen and some metals.

Meteorites found on Antarctica may have come from Mars, and some appear to contain fossilized bacteria.

On some coastlines made up of soft rocks, the sea carves away metres of land every year. Some villages, such as Dunwich in Suffolk, England, have partly vanished into the sea as cliffs collapsed beneath them due to erosion.

Ice has the power to shatter rock. Granite, one of the hardest rocks, can be split by water in cracks expanding as it freezes. The combined weight and movement of a glacier (a river of ice) can hollow out a whole mountainside.

Unaware that it was poisonous, women in ancient Rome used the mineral arsenic as a cosmetic to whiten their skin.

Graphite, the soft mineral used in pencil leads, is also used in nuclear power stations. Huge graphite rods help to control the speed of nuclear reactions in the reactor core.

Obsidian is a black, volcanic rock that is so shiny that people in ancient times used to use it as mirror. The rock also forms such sharp edges when it is broken that it was also used to make cutting tools.

Obsidian

Rocks are constantly changing, usually very, very slowly, due to erosion and forces deep inside the Earth. It has taken millions of years for water and wind to carve out this sandstone arch (right).

Rock arch in
Utah, USA

Fossil of *Archaeopteryx*

In 1861, a quarryman split open a block of limestone and discovered the fossil of a bird-like creature with feathers that lived 150 million years ago. This creature, which scientists called *Archaeopteryx*, may be the link between prehistoric reptiles and the birds of today.

Minerals don't just exist in rocks. Your bones are made of minerals, too!

QUESTIONS AND ANSWERS

Q What are the most common rocks in the Earth's crust?

A Volcanic rocks, such as basalt, are the most common rocks in the Earth's crust. Basalt forms from the more fluid type of lava as it cools and hardens. It makes up the ocean floors, which cover 68% of the Earth's surface.

Q How do we know that dinosaurs existed?

A Dinosaur bones and teeth have been found as fossils in rocks all around the world. In some places, even their footprints and dung have been preserved in rock. It is mainly from fossils that we know about plants and animals that lived on Earth in the past.

Fossilized footprint of a dinosaur

Chinese nephrite dragon.

Q What is jade, and why has it got more than one name?

A People once thought there was a single green stone called jade. But, in 1863, this rock was found to be two different minerals, now called jadeite and nephrite.

Q Why are the pebbles on a beach so many different colours?

A Pebbles are made up of many different types of rock. Their colours show what kinds of minerals they contain. The pebbles on one beach may have been washed there by the sea from several different places.

Q Why is the sand black on some beaches around the world?

A Sand is made from rocks and pebbles that have been worn down into fine grains. In some places, such as the Canary Islands, the sand is black because it is made of volcanic ash rich in dark minerals.

Q If pumice is a rock how come it can float on water?

A Pumice is hardened lava froth. It is full of tiny air bubbles; the air trapped inside these bubbles makes the pumice light enough to float on water.

Q What made the stripes on the rocks in Utah, USA?

A The desert rocks are made of layers of sandstone. Hot days, cold nights, floods and storms have worn away the softer layers of rock the fastest, creating stripes in the landscape.

Q What are the oldest rocks on Earth?

A The oldest known rocks came from outer space as meteorites. This piece of chondrite (right) is a meteorite that is about 4,600 million years old. The first rocks to form on Earth didn't develop until later on, about 4,200 million years ago.

Chondrite

Q Where do new rocks come from?

A New rocks are forming all the time, on the surface of the Earth and deep in its crust. Some rocks are made from layers of sediment. Others are the result of volcanic activity, both on the ocean floors and above ground. The Earth constantly recycles rocks by means of heat, pressure and erosion.

Q What is a desert rose made from and how did it form?

A A desert rose is made of a mineral called gypsum. It formed in a desert when water evaporated quickly. Impurities from the water were left behind and formed crystals shaped like petals.

Desert rose

Record Breakers

MOST VALUABLE METAL
Platinum is currently the most valuable metal, more valuable than gold.

BIGGEST GOLD NUGGET
The largest gold nugget ever found weighed 70.9 kg (156.3 lb), that's as heavy as a man.

MOST VALUABLE RELIGIOUS ITEM
The Golden Buddha of Bangkok is the most valuable religious item in the world. It is made of 5.5 tonnes (6.1 tons) of solid gold.

HARDEST MINERAL
Diamond is the hardest known mineral and cannot be scratched by any other mineral.

BIGGEST STALAGMITE
The biggest stalagmite is in Krasnohorska, Slovakia. It is 31.5 m (105 ft) tall.

BIGGEST ROCK
Uluru (Ayer's Rock) in Australia is the biggest freestanding rock in the world. It is over 3.6 km (2 miles) long.

Badlands, Utah, USA

Rock or mineral?

GEOLOGISTS CLASSIFY ROCKS according to the way in which they were formed. There are three main types of rock: igneous, metamorphic and sedimentary rocks. Below you can find out about the main characteristics of each type.

Geologist's tools

IDENTIFYING ROCKS

IGNEOUS ROCKS
Igneous rocks are made from hot, molten rock from deep within the Earth that has solidified as it has cooled. Like metamorphic rocks, they are made of interlocking crystals of different minerals. The more slowly a rock has cooled and solidified, the larger the crystals that have formed within it.

Large grains of quartz, feldspar and mica formed as the rock cooled slowly

Granite

Large crystals that formed as the rock cooled slowly

Gabbro

Dark, fine-grains that formed from volcanic lava

Basalt

Very fine-grained, glassy texture

Obsidian

METAMORPHIC ROCKS
Entirely new metamorphic rocks are formed when igneous or sedimentary rocks undergo a complete transformation as a result of heat and pressure within the Earth's crust. The minerals in a metamorphic rock usually form crystals of a size that reflects the degree of heat and pressure they underwent.

Wavy, folded appearance

Folded schist

Fine grain size

Slate

Dark and light foliated bands of colour

Gneiss

SEDIMENTARY ROCKS
Sedimentary rocks are usually made from particles that have been weathered and eroded from other rocks. Over time, these particles, which range from the size of sand grains to that of boulders, are deposited in layers (strata) and become rocks. Sedimentary rocks are the ones that most commonly contain fossils.

Large, coarse particles cemented together

Conglomerate

Iron oxide gives orange colour

Sandstone

Angular fragments of rock held together by a fine, sandy material

Breccia

Soft, powdery texture formed from the skeletons of micro-organisms

Chalk

IDENTIFYING MINERALS

No two minerals are the same, and many have a particular colour or shape that will help in identifying them. Some form large crystals; others form bubbly masses or grow as crusts on rocks. Below is a sample of minerals and their distinguishing features.

Prismatic beryl crystal

BERYL
Beryl forms deep within the Earth's crust and is found mainly in granites and pegmatites. Transparent beryl is hard and rare, making it a valuable gemstone. It has different names, depending on its colour. Green emerald and blue-green aquamarine are the best-known varieties.

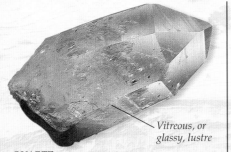

Vitreous, or glassy, lustre

QUARTZ
One of the most common minerals, quartz occurs in many rocks and is often found in mineral veins with metal ores. Quartz crystals usually have six sides with a top shaped like a pyramid. Clear, transparent quartz is often called rock crystal and is sometimes mistaken for diamond.

GOLD
Gold is a metal and a rare native element. It is usually found as yellow specks in rocks and often grows with quartz in mineral veins when hot, watery liquids cool. Gold occasionally forms large crystalline nuggets with rounded edges.

Sapphire crystals joined with tourmaline

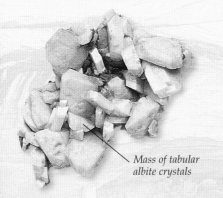

Mass of tabular albite crystals

ALBITE
Albite is an important variety of feldspar, a rock-forming mineral, and is often found in granites, schists and sandstones. It is most usually made up of grains, rather than well-formed crystals, and is white or colourless.

Pearly lustre on crystals

COCKSCOMB BARITE
Despite its crystalline form, barite is heavier than some metallic minerals. It forms in many environments, from hot volcanic springs to mineral veins. Cockscomb barite is made up of rounded masses of soft, plate-like crystals.

CORUNDUM
Although the pure form of corundum is colourless, it comes in many colours. Rubies and sapphires are both rare forms and are most commonly found in river gravels. Corundum is extremely hard and forms crystals of different shapes.

CALCITE
Calcite forms limestone rock and also develops in sea water and in bone and shell. It is the mineral that forms stalactites and stalagmites. As well as forming crystals, it can be granular, fibrous and massive.

Flat-topped, bright yellow crystal

SULPHUR
A native element, sulphur crystallizes around hot springs and volcanic craters. It sometimes forms a powdery crust of small crystals, but large crystals are also common. Pure crystals are always yellow and are soft enough to be cut with a knife.

Orange halite crystals

HALITE
Halite belongs to a range of minerals called evaporites, which form when salty water evaporates. It occurs around seas and lakes in dry climates and is best known as rock salt. It is usually found in masses but also forms single, cube-shaped crystals.

Find out more

YOU CAN GO ROCK AND MINERAL collecting almost anywhere. Rocks are all around you, not just on the ground, but in walls, buildings and sculptures. The best way to find out more about them is to collect them. There are suggestions for where to start looking on the left. Many museums have extensive rock collections and are a good source of information. Going on a trip or holiday can also provide valuable opportunities to find different rocks and discover new types of landscape. Here you will find suggestions for good places to visit, as well as a list of useful websites that can provide plenty more information.

COLLECTING ROCKS AND MINERALS
Pebble beaches are good places to search for specimens. To start with, look for pebbles in different colours, and see how many types you can find. Other interesting places to look are lakesides and river banks, but always remember to take care.

GATHERING INFORMATION
Visit your nearest natural history or geological museum to see collections of rocks and minerals, both rare and common, and to find out how the rocks were formed. Many museums have interactive displays and lots of information on volcanoes, earthquakes and rocks from space.

Places to visit

THE EARTH GALLERIES AT THE NATURAL HISTORY MUSEUM, LONDON
Cromwell Road,
London SW7 5BD

NATIONAL MUSEUM OF WALES
Cathays Park,
Cardiff CF1 3NP

ROYAL MUSEUM OF SCOTLAND
Chambers Street,
Edinburgh EH1 1JF

TRINITY COLLEGE GEOLOGICAL MUSEUM, IRELAND
Department of Geology,
Trinity College, Dublin 2

Earth Lab

IDENTIFYING SPECIMENS
You can take your rock samples to some museums for help in identifying them. At the Earth Lab in the Earth Galleries at the Natural History Museum in London, there are over 2,000 specimens of rocks, minerals and fossils. You can identify your own specimens, examine materials with the Lab microscopes and consult qualified staff about your finds.

DISPLAYING YOUR COLLECTION
Gently clean your rock samples with water and let them dry, then arrange them in empty matchboxes or small cardboard trays. For delicate items, line the trays with tissue paper. Put a small data card in the base of each tray, with the specimen's name, where you found it and the date you found it. Group the specimens in a tray or drawer, arranging them by colour or by the places where you found them.

Cardboard trays lined with tissue

Specimen labels

GEMSTONES AND JEWELLERY

Attractive stones, such as jade, have been carved to make decorative objects for centuries. A good place to look for jewellery and other objects carved from rock is at a museum of decorative arts, such as the Victoria and Albert Museum, in London.

Aztec jade necklace

HISTORY IN THE ROCKS

Visitors to the Grand Canyon, in Arizona, USA, have a spectacular view of different layers of the Earth's rocks. The canyon was carved out by the Colorado River and took several million years to form. As the river cut its way downwards, it exposed different layers of rock that had been hidden beneath the ground. The rocks are mostly sandstones and limestones and contain bands of fossils from different geological periods. Going down the steep trails to the bottom of the gorge is like travelling back in time through the history of the rocks.

The Grand Canyon

SCULPTURES

The Ancient Greeks and Romans used marble to create their finest statues and buildings because it was ideal for carving. Pure marble is white and is smooth and shiny when polished. Look at statues closely to find out whether they are made from marble or another type of stone.

Marble statue of Pieta, St Patrick's Cathedral, New York

GIANT'S STEPS

At the Giant's Causeway in Antrim, Northern Ireland, visitors can see extraordinary columns of rock up to 2 m (7 ft) tall stacked closely together. According to legend, giants built it as a stepping-stone pathway across the sea. Geologists, however, say the causeway was made when basalt lava cooled and shrank evenly, forming hexagonal basalt columns.

Cave at Melissani, Cephalonia, Greece

LIMESTONE CAVES AND GROTTOS

Limestone caves are good places to see stalactites that look like giant icicles and brilliant turquoise waters. There are blue grottos at several islands in the Mediterranean, such as Cephalonia in Greece. Famous limestone caves include the Lascaux Caves in France, where you can also see prehistoric cave paintings.

Glossary

ABRASION Erosion caused by water, wind or ice laden with sediments scraping or rubbing against the surface of rocks.

ACICULAR A term used to describe minerals composed of crystals that are needle-like in shape.

ALLOY A metallic material, such as brass, bronze or steel, that is a mixture of two different types of metal.

CABOCHON A gemstone cut in which the stone has a smooth domed upper surface without any facets.

CARAT The standard measure of weight for precious stones. One metric carat equals 0.2 g. The term is also used to describe the purity of gold; pure gold is 24 carat.

CLEAVAGE The way in which a crystal splits apart along certain well-defined planes according to its internal structure.

CORE The area of iron and nickel that makes up the centre of the Earth. It is about 1,370 km (850 miles) in diameter.

CRUST The thin outer layer of the Earth. It varies in thickness between 7 and 70 km (4 and 43½ miles).

CRYSTAL A naturally occurring solid with a regular internal structure and smooth external faces.

Group of natural crystals

CRYSTALLIZE To form crystals, or to make them form.

DEBRIS Scattered broken fragments of material formed by weathering and erosion.

DENDRITIC Having a branch-like form.

DEPOSIT A gradual build up of sediments.

ELEMENT One of the basic substances from which all matter is made. An element cannot be broken down into a simpler substance.

EROSION The wearing away of the Earth's surface by processes involving movement, such as that of rivers and glaciers.

Ground worn away by erosion

EVAPORITE Mineral or rock formed as a result of salt or spring water evaporating.

EXTRUSIVE ROCK Rock that is formed when magma erupts from the Earth as lava and cools on reaching the surface.

FACE A surface of a crystal.

FACET One side of a cut gemstone.

FIRE A term used for dispersed light. A gem with strong fire, such as a diamond, is unusually bright.

FOLIATION Wavy patterns caused by aligned crystals in metamorphic rocks.

FOSSIL The remains or traces of plants or animals that have been preserved in the Earth's crust. They may be in rock, amber, permafrost or tar pits. Even the impressions of delicate leaves, feathers or skin as well as traces such as footprints are considered to be fossils.

GALVANIZATION A process by which zinc is added to other metals or alloys to prevent them from rusting.

GEMSTONE Naturally occurring minerals, usually in crystal form, that are valued for their beauty, rarity and hardness.

Ammonite fossil

GEOLOGIST A person who studies rocks and minerals to find out about the structure of the Earth's crust and how it formed.

HABIT The shape, size and general appearance of a crystal or group of crystals.

HOPPER CRYSTALS Crystals that have regular, stepped cavities in each face.

INTRUSIVE ROCKS Igneous rocks that solidify within the Earth's crust and only appear at the surface once the rocks lying on top of them have eroded away.

IRIDESCENCE A rainbow-like play of colours on the surface of a mineral, similar to that of a film of oil on water.

KARST SCENERY The characteristic broken rock formations of some limestone plateaus.

LAPIDARY A professional craftsman skilled at cutting gemstones to obtain the best optical effect.

LAVA Red-hot, molten rock (magma) from deep within the Earth that erupts to the surface from volcanoes and other vents.

LUSTRE The way in which a mineral shines. It is affected by the way that light is reflected from the surface of the mineral.

MAGMA Molten rock below the surface of the Earth.

MANTLE The layer of the Earth between the core and the crust. It is about 2,900 km (1,800 miles) thick.

MASSIVE A term used to describe a mineral that has no definite shape.

MATRIX A mass of rock in which crystals are set.

METAMORPHOSE To undergo a change of structure and composition. In rocks, this is usually caused by the action of heat or pressure.

METEORITE An object from outer space, such as a rock, that survives the passage through the atmosphere to reach Earth.

MINERAL A naturally occurring, inorganic solid with certain definite characteristics, such as crystal structure and chemical composition.

Diamond

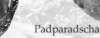

Padparadscha

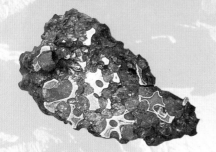

Meteorite

MINERAL VEIN A crack in rocks in which minerals from hot fluids have been deposited.

MOHS' SCALE A scale, devised by the Austrian mineralogist Friedrich Mohs, that measures the hardness of minerals according to what they can scratch.

MOLTEN Melted, made into a liquid by great heat, especially with reference to rocks.

NATIVE ELEMENT An element that occurs naturally in a free state and does not form part of a compound.

NODULE A rounded lump of mineral found in sedimentary rock.

OOLITH Small, rounded grains that make up some sedimentary rocks.

OPAQUE Material that does not let light pass through it.

OPTICAL PROPERTIES The various optical effects produced as light passes through minerals. This is one of the properties used to help identify minerals.

ORE A rock or mineral from which a metal can be extracted.

OUTCROP The whole area that one type of rock covers on a geological map, including the parts covered by soil or buildings.

PALAEONTOLOGIST A scientist who studies fossils.

PIGMENT A natural colouring material often used in paints and dyes. Many pigments were originally made by crushing coloured rocks and mixing the powders with animal fats.

Azurite, once ground into a prized blue pigment

POROUS Able to absorb water, air or other fluids.

PORPHYRY An igneous rock containing fairly large crystals set into a finer matrix.

PRECIPITATION A chemical process during which a solid substance, such as lime, is deposited from a solution, such as lime-rich water.

PYROCLASTIC ROCK Pyroclastic means "fire-broken" and describes all the fragments of rock, pumice and solid lava that may be erupted from a volcano.

Stalactites hanging from the roof of a cave

RESIN A sticky substance that comes from some plants.

ROCK An aggregate of mineral particles.

SEDIMENT Rock material of various sizes, ranging from boulders to silt, which is the product of weathering and erosion, as well as shell fragments and other organic material.

SMELTING The process by which ore is melted to extract the metal that it contains.

SPECIFIC GRAVITY A property of minerals that relates a mineral's chemical composition to its crystal structure. It is defined by comparing the weight of a mineral with the weight of an equal volume of water.

STALACTITE An irregular, hanging spike made of calcium carbonate (lime) formed as dripping water precipitates lime from the roof of a cave. Over a long period of time, stony stalactites build up in size and may hang many metres from a cave roof.

STALAGMITE A stony spike standing like a tapering post on the base of a limestone cave. Stalagmites form where water has dripped from the roof of the cave or a stalactite above, slowly building up lime deposits.

STREAK The colour produced when a mineral is crushed into a fine powder. The colour of a streak is used to help identify minerals. It is often a better means of identification than the colour of the mineral itself, as it is less variable.

STRIATIONS Parallel scratches, grooves or lines on a crystal face that develop as the crystal grows.

SWALLOW HOLE A hollow in the ground, especially in limestone, where a surface stream disappears from sight and flows underground.

TRANSLUCENT Material that allows some light to pass through it, but is not clear.

TRANSPARENT Material that allows light to pass through it. It can be seen through.

TUMBLING The process of rolling rough mineral pieces in a tumbling machine with grit and water until the pebbles are rounded and polished.

VEIN A thin layer or deposit of mineral or ore between larger layers of a different rock or mineral.

Veins of calcite

VESICLE A gas bubble or cavity in lava that is left as a hole after the lava has cooled down and solidified.

VOLCANIC BOMB A blob of lava that is thrown out of a volcano and solidifies before hitting the ground.

VOLCANIC VENT The central passage in a volcano through which magma flows and erupts as lava.

WEATHERING The breaking down of rocks on the Earth's surface. This is mainly a chemical reaction, aided by the presence of water, but it may also be due to processes such as alternate freezing and thawing.

Index

AB

acid lavas, 18,19
agate, 52, 53, 60, 61
agglomerates, 18
Akrotiri, 19
albite, 67
aluminium, 56
amber, 14, 64
amthyst, 55, 61
ammonites, 20, 39
amphiboles, 42
anthracite, 7, 37
apatite, 45, 49
aquamarine, 67
arsenic, 64
asteroids, 41
augite, 8, 17, 43
azurite, 33, 45
barite, 67
baryte, 45, 48
basalt, 8, 9, 10, 16, 17, 19, 64, 65, 66, 69
basic lavas, 18, 19
bauxite, 13, 56
beaches, 65, 68
beryl, 45, 46, 50, 67
biotite, 8, 16, 25, 42
Black Prince's ruby, 54
bone, 64, 67
bornite, 56
breccia, 18, 21, 27, 66
bricks, 15, 35
building stones, 34-35

CD

calcite, 8, 17, 20, 22-3, 24, 45, 47, 48, 49, 67
cameos, 53, 61
carbon, 24, 41, 48
carbonates, 43
Carrara marble, 26, 27
cassiterite, 6, 57
cave paintings, 32
caves, limestone, 22-3, 69
cement, 35
chalcanthite, 9
chalcedony, 42, 52-3
chalcopyrite, 32, 46, 47, 56, 59

chalk, 15, 20, 32, 66
charcoal, 32
chemical weathering, 13
chondrite, 65
cinnabar, 32, 33, 57
citrine, 6
clays, 11, 13, 21, 32, 35, 43
claystone, 9, 11
cleavage, 48
coal, 7, 36-7
coastal erosion, 64
cockscomb barite, 67
collecting, 62-3
colour, pigments, 32
concretion, 9
conglomerate, 21, 31, 66
copper, 33, 47, 56
core, Earth's, 6
corundum, 45, 59, 62, 67
crust, Earth's, 6, 10, 64, 65
crystals, 6, 44-7, 66, 67
cutting gemstones, 60-1
desert rose, 65
deserts, 11, 12
diamonds, 6, 48, 49, 50, 60, 65
dinosaurs, 65
diorite, 30, 42
dreikanters, 12

EF

Earth, structure, 6, 64, 65
Ease Gill Carves, 22
eclogite, 25
emeralds, 50, 60, 67
Empire State Building, 36
erosion, 12-13, 64
evaporites, 7, 9, 21, 67
extrusive rocks, 16
feldspars, 8, 10, 11, 13, 16-17, 24, 41, 42, 66, 67
feldspathoids, 43
flint, 15, 20, 21; tools, 28-9
flurorite, 49
formation of rocks, 10-11
fossils, 6, 14, 34, 38-9, 64, 65, 66

GH

gabbro, 10, 17, 66
galena, 48, 49, 57
garnet, 24, 25, 46, 54-55
gemstones, 6, 50-5, 60-1, 69

Giant's Causeway, 16, 17, 69
glaciers, 13
gneiss, 10, 11, 25, 66
gold, 6, 58, 59, 64, 65, 67
goniometer, 45
gossan, 13
Grand Canyon, 21, 69
granite, 7, 8, 10, 13, 15, 16, 35, 42, 64, 66, 67
graphite, 48, 64
Great Wall of China, 35
grit, 21
gypsum, 21, 45, 49, 65
habits, crystal, 46-7
halite, 21, 47, 67
Halley's comet, 43
hardness, 49
hematite, 32, 33, 46, 56
hornblende, 11, 42
hornfels, 24

IJK

ice, 13, 64
identifying rocks and minerals, 66-7
igneous rocks, 7, 10, 11, 16-17, 42, 66
intaglios, 61
intrusive rocks, 16
iron, 56; meteorites, 40, 41
jade, 52, 53, 65, 69
jadeite, 53, 65
jet, 36
kaolin, 32, 43
karst scenery, 23
Kilimanjaro, Mount, 7
kimberlite, 6, 50
Koh-i-noor, 50

LM

labradorite, 8
lapis lazuli, 33, 52
lava, 7, 10, 17, 18-19, 64, 65, 66, 69
lead, 48, 57
lignite, 37
limestone, 6, 7, 20, 24, 34-5, 64, 67; caves, 22-3, 69; pavements, 22
magma, 6, 7, 10, 16, 18
magnetism, 49
magnetite, 15, 49

malachite, 33
man-made building stones, 35
mantle, Earth's, 6, 10
marble, 8, 24, 26-7, 39, 69
Mars, 41, 64
mercury, 57
metals, 56-9, 67; precious, 6, 58-9
metamorphic rocks, 10, 11, 24-5, 66
meteorites, 40-1, 64, 65
mica, 8, 11, 14, 24, 25, 42, 46, 49, 66
migmatites, 10, 25
Mississippi River, 11
Mohs' scale, 49
Monument Valley, 12
Moon rocks, 41, 64
mountain-building, 6, 24

NO

nephrite, 53, 65
nickel, 57
nile, River, 7
nodules, 9, 14, 15
norite, 9
Notre Dame, 35
nuclear reactors, 64
obsidian, 16, 19, 29, 64, 66
ocean floors, 65
oil shale, 36
olivine, 8, 9, 15, 17, 19, 40, 43, 45, 54
onion-skin weathering, 12
oolitic limestone, 20, 34
opals, 51
optical properties, 49
ore minerals, 6, 56-7
orpiment, 32, 33
orthoclase, 8, 42, 45, 49

PQ

Pamukkale Falls, 23
Parthenon, 13
peat, 37
pebbles, 6, 14-15, 65, 68
Pelée, Mount, 9
"Pele's hair", 9
pegmatite, 67
peridot, 8, 54
periodotite, 17
pigments, 32-3

pitchstone, 16
plagioclase feldspar, 8, 9, 17, 43, 45
platinum, 6, 58, 65
plutonic see intrusive rocks
Pompeii, 19
porphyry, 17
Portland stone, 34
precious metals, 6, 58-9
properties of minerals, 48-9
pumice, 19, 65
Puy de Dôme, 10
Pyramids, 34
pyrite, 6, 15, 45, 47, 59
pyroclastic rocks, 7, 18
pyroxene, 8, 9, 17, 19, 24, 25, 40, 41, 43, 66
pyrrhotine, 49
quartz, 8, 16, 24, 42, 59, 66, 67; crystals, 6, 44, 45, 47; formation, 11; pebbles, 15; polishing, 61; properties, 48, 49; sand, 14
quartzite, 6, 8, 11, 14, 24, 30

RS

realgar, 33
rhyolite, 19, 30
rivers, 11
rock crystal, 44, 61, 67
rock salt, 21, 47, 67
ropy lavas, 7, 19
rose, quartz, 61
rubies, 51, 67
rutile, 56
St Helens, Mount, 18, 19
salt, 21, 47, 67
sand, 9, 12, 14-15, 47, 65
sandstone, 11, 12, 14, 21, 35, 64, 65, 66
sapphires, 51, 67
schists, 10, 11, 14, 25, 66
seashores, 14-15, 64, 65
sedimentary rocks, 7, 10, 11, 20-1, 38, 66
sediments, 12, 13, 20, 38
serpentinite, 17
shale, 21
shells, 6, 14, 20, 38-9, 67
siderite, 45
silica, 20, 42
silicates, 64

silver, 66, 58
slate, 14, 24, 25, 34
specific gravity, 49
sperrylite, 58
sphalerite, 47, 57
spinels, 54
slate, 66
stalactites, 9, 22, 23, 67
stalagmites, 23, 65, 67
stibnite, 48
structure, Earth's, 6
Sugar Loaf Mountain, 10
sulphur, 67
swallow holes, 22
symmetry, crystal, 45

T

Taj Mahal, 27
talc, 49
temperature, weathering, 12
thomsonite, 61
till, 13
tin, 6, 57
titanium, 56
tools, 28-31, 62-63
topaz, 45, 49, 54
torrs, 13
tourmaline, 32, 45, 54, 55
travertine, 23, 27
tremolite, 42, 46
tufa, 21, 22, 27
tuff, 18, 30
tumbling, 60-1
turquoise, 52
twin crystals, 45

UVWZ

unakite, 61
vesicular volcanic rocks, 17
Vesuvius, 19
volcanic ash, 15, 18, 21, 65
volcanic rocks, 7, 17, 18-19, 64, 65, 66
volcanoes, 10, 18-19, 64, 65
weathering, 10, 11, 12-13
whetstones, 31
wind erosion, 12
wulfenite, 9, 45
zinc, 57
zircon, 45, 54

Acknowledgements

Dorling Kindersley would like to thank:
Dr Wendy Kirck of University College London; the staff of the British Museum (Natural History); and Gavin Morgan, Nick Merryman and Christine Jones at the Museum of London for their advice and invaluable help in providing specimens.
Redland Brick Company and Jacobson Hirsch for the loan of equipment.
Anne-marie Bulat for her work on the initial stages of the book.
David Nixon for design assistance, and Tim Hammond for editorial assistance.
Fred Ford and Mike Pilley of Radius Graphics, and Ray Owen and Nick Madren for artwork.

Picture credits
t=top b=bottom m=middle l=left r=right

Ardea London Ltd: Francois Gohier 65t
Didier Barrault / Robert Harding Picture Library: 37mr
Bridgeman Art Library / Bonhoms,

London: 55mr
Paul Brierley: 49b; 51m
British Museum (Natural History): 42m; 43
N. A. Callow / Robert Harding Picture Library: 13b
Bruce Coleman Ltd: Derek Croucher 69br; Jeff Foott 65bl; Natural Selection Inc 64br
G. & P. Corrigan / Robert Harding Picture Library: 23t
GeoScience Features Picture Library: 68tr
Diamond information Centre: 60m
C. M. Dixon / Photoresources: 11b; 14t; 15t; 19b; 32b
Earth Satellite Corporation / Science Photo Library: 7t
Mary Evans Picture Library: 6t; 8; 9m; 12b; 15b; 16tl; 19t; 25; 26b; 28b; 30bl; 31b; 32t; 34t, ml; 36t; 37t, bl; 39b; 40t; 41t; 44tr; 50tr, br; 56mr; 57m; 58tl, tr; 59tl, b; 62t, m
Clive Friend / Woodmansterne Ltd.: 15m, 36b
Jon Gardey / Robert Harding Picture Library: 40b

Geoscience Features: 18t
Mike Gray / University College London: 17; 20tr; 24tf
Ian Griffiths / Robert Harding Picture Library: 13t
Robert Harding Picture Library: 13m; 18br; 21; 22bl; 23m; 27t, b; 35t, b; 56t; 59m
Brian Hawkes / Robert Harding Picture Library: 12m
Michael Holford: 50tl, bl; 51t; 54t, mr; 55t, ml
Glenn I. Huss: 40m
The Hutchinson Library: 35m; 51b; 56ml
INAH: Michel Zabé 69tr
Yoram Lehmann/Robert Harding Picture Library: 37ml
Kenneth Lucas / Planet Earth: 39t
Johnson Matthey: 58bl
Museum of London: 28t; 32m; 61tl, br
NASA:
NASA/Robert Harding Picture Library: 6-7, 7b
NASA / Spectrum Colour Library: 11t
National Coal Board: 37br
The Natural History Museum, London: 68cl, 68cr, 71clrb
N.H.P.A.: Kevin Schafer 64cl
Walter Rawlings / Robert Harding Picture

Library: 26m; 33b
John G. Ross/Robert Harding Picture Library: 53
K. Scholz / ZEFA: 10b
Nicholas Servian /Woodmansterne: 34mr
A. Sorrell / Museum of London: 29t
Spectrum Colour Library: 10m
R. F. Symes: 9tr
A. C. Waltham / Robert Harding Picture Library: 22br
Werner Forman Archive: 29b; 30br; 31tl, ml; 52t, b, 55b; 61m
G. M. Wilkins / Robert Harding Picture Library: 47
Woodmansterne: 58br
ZEFA: 16tr
Zeiss: 41bl
Reproduced with the premission of the Controller of Her Majesty's Stationery Office, Crown copyright: 54ml

Jacket credits:
Mary Evans Picture Library: back ca
Natural History Museum back, back c, back cl, back cr, front tr

Illustrations: Andrew Macdonald 6m, b; 14ml; 18bl; 22ml; 28mr; 30mr.